GREEK
TRAGEDIES

VOLUME

3

AESCHYLUS

THE EUMENIDES

Translated by Richmond Lattimore

SOPHOCLES

PHILOCTETES

Translated by David Grene

OEDIPUS AT COLONUS

Translated by David Grene

EURIPIDES

THE BACCHAE

Translated by William Arrowsmith

ALCESTIS

Translated by Richmond Lattimore

GREEK TRAGEDIES

Edited by

DAVID GRENE *and* RICHMOND LATTIMORE

VOLUME

3

Second Edition

THE UNIVERSITY OF CHICAGO PRESS

CHICAGO & LONDON

THE UNIVERSITY OF CHICAGO PRESS, CHICAGO 60637
The University of Chicago Press, Ltd., London

Second edition published 1991 by The University of Chicago Press
Printed in the United States of America

00 99 98 97 96 95 94
10 9 8 7 6 5 4 3

Library of Congress Cataloging-in-Publication Data

Greek tragedies / edited by David Grene and Richmond Lattimore.
—2nd ed.
p. cm.
Translated from Greek.
Selections from the Greek tragedies published in 1960 by the University of Chicago Press.
ISBN 0-226-30791-3 (pbk.)
1. Greek drama (Tragedy)—Translations into English. 2. English drama (Tragedy)—Translations from Greek. I. Grene, David. II. Lattimore, Richmond Alexander, 1906–1984.
PA3626.A2G7 1991
882′.0108—dc20 90-49984
CIP

⊗ The paper used in this publication meets the minimum requirements of the American National Standard for Information Sciences—Permanence of Paper for Printed Library Materials, ANSI Z39.48-1984.

PUBLISHER'S NOTE

In this edition of *Greek Tragedies,* volume 3, Robert Fitzgerald's 1941 translation of *Oedipus at Colonus* has been replaced with a new translation by David Grene.

Except for the translator's note to *Oedipus at Colonus* by David Grene, the brief introductions to the plays in this volume were written by Richmond Lattimore, who wrote, "As befits a limited volume, I have tried to state, very briefly, the essential features of each tragedy here reprinted. The personal views given are, of course, my own, and the translators, other than myself, are not to be held responsible."

Longer and fuller introductions, mostly by the translators themselves, will be found in *The Complete Greek Tragedies,* edited by David Grene and Richmond Lattimore. The complete collection of Greek tragedies is available in nine paperback volumes (of which there is a list at the end of this volume).

CONTENTS

THE EUMENIDES

Translated by Richmond Lattimore

INTRODUCTION

The Eumenides was presented in 458 B.C. as the last tragedy in the trilogy called *The Oresteia*. The other plays in the trilogy are *Agamemnon* and *The Libation Bearers*. Each of the three can be studied and interpreted as an independent drama, in isolation from the other two.

When Orestes murdered his mother, he did so by command of Apollo, but even Apollo could not by formal absolution drive away the Furies of the Mother (ultimately canonized as the Eumenides), who pursued the murderer up and down the world. At last the case was brought to Athens and tried by law, before a jury of twelve Athenian citizens, with Athene presiding as judge and Apollo as counsel for the defense. With the count six to six, Athene gave her casting vote for mercy and acquittal, and appeased the Eumenides by establishing them in the place of their subsequent cult, as guardian spirits of Athens.

As a drama of atonement, absolution, and canonization, *The Eumenides* bears some resemblance to Sophocles' *Oedipus at Colonus*. In both cases the hero, morally blameless, is nevertheless contaminated and must be absolved. But Sophocles keeps his supernatural powers in the background. Aeschylus stages his; and his issues are public, not individual, as the story of the Argive House of Atreus in its solution merges into the history of civilization at Athens, which represents in fact the world's progress. Through Athene and the reconciled Eumenides, Aeschylus unmistakably speaks his mind to the Athenians in the stately conclusion of *The Oresteia*.

NOTE

The translation of this play is based on H. W. Smyth's "Loeb Classical Library" text (London and New York: William Heinemann, Ltd., and G. P. Putnam's Sons, 1926). A few deviations from this text occur where the translator has followed the manuscript readings instead of emendations accepted by Smyth.

Various editions of Greek drama divide the lines of lyric passages in various ways, but editors regularly follow the traditional line numbers whether their own line divisions tally with these numbers or not. This accounts for what may appear to be erratic line numbering in this translation, for instance, line 360 and following. The line numbering in this translation is that of Smyth's text.

CHARACTERS

Priestess of Apollo, the Pythia

Apollo

Hermes (silent)

Ghost of Clytaemestra

Orestes

Athene

Chorus of Eumenides (Furies)

Second Chorus; women of Athens

Jurymen, herald, citizens of Athens (all silent parts)

THE EUMENIDES

SCENE: *For the first part of the play [1–234) the scene is Delphi, before the sanctuary of Pythian Apollo. The action of the rest of the play (235 to the end) takes place at Athens, on the Acropolis before the temple of Athene. A simple change in the backdrop will indicate the shift.*

(Enter, alone, the Pythia.)

Pythia

I give first place of honor in my prayer to her
who of the gods first prophesied, the Earth; and next
to Themis, who succeeded to her mother's place
of prophecy; so runs the legend; and in third
succession, given by free consent, not won by force,
another Titan daughter of Earth was seated here.
This was Phoebe. She gave it as a birthday gift
to Phoebus, who is called still after Phoebe's name.
And he, leaving the pond of Delos and the reef,
grounded his ship at the roadstead of Pallas, then
made his way to this land and a Parnassian home.
Deep in respect for his degree Hephaestus' sons
conveyed him here, for these are builders of roads, and changed
the wilderness to a land that was no wilderness.
He came so, and the people highly honored him,
with Delphus, lord and helmsman of the country. Zeus
made his mind full with godship and prophetic craft
and placed him, fourth in a line of seers, upon this throne.
So, Loxias is the spokesman of his father, Zeus.
These are the gods I set in the proem of my prayer.
But Pallas-before-the-temple has her right in all
I say. I worship the nymphs where the Corycian rock
is hollowed inward, haunt of birds and paced by gods.
Bromius, whom I forget not, sways this place. From here
in divine form he led his Bacchanals in arms

to hunt down Pentheus like a hare in the deathtrap.
I call upon the springs of Pleistus, on the power
of Poseidon, and on final loftiest Zeus,
then go to sit in prophecy on the throne. May all
grant me that this of all my entrances shall be
the best by far. If there are any Hellenes here
let them draw lots, so enter, as the custom is.
My prophecy is only as the god may guide.

(She enters the temple and almost immediately comes out again.)

Things terrible to tell and for the eyes to see
terrible drove me out again from Loxias' house
so that I have no strength and cannot stand on springing
feet, but run with hands' help and my legs have no speed.
An old woman afraid is nothing: a child, no more.
See, I am on my way to the wreath-hung recess
and on the centrestone I see a man with god's
defilement on him postured in the suppliant's seat
with blood dripping from his hands and from a new-drawn sword,
holding too a branch that had grown high on an olive
tree, decorously wrapped in a great tuft of wool,
and the fleece shone. So far, at least, I can speak clear.
In front of this man slept a startling company
of women lying all upon the chairs. Or not
women, I think I call them rather gorgons, only
not gorgons either, since their shape is not the same.
I saw some creatures painted in a picture once,
who tore the food from Phineus, only these had no
wings, that could be seen; they are black and utterly
repulsive, and they snore with breath that drives one back.
From their eyes drips the foul ooze, and their dress is such
as is not right to wear in the presence of the gods'
statues, nor even into any human house.
I have never seen the tribe that owns this company
nor know what piece of earth can claim with pride it bore

such brood, and without hurt and tears for labor given.
Now after this the master of the house must take
his own measures: Apollo Loxias, who is very strong
and heals by divination; reads portentous signs,
and so clears out the houses others hold as well.

(Exit. The doors of the temple open and show Orestes surrounded by the sleeping Furies, Apollo and Hermes beside him.)

Apollo

I will not give you up. Through to the end standing
your guardian, whether by your side or far away,
I shall not weaken toward your enemies. See now
how I have caught and overpowered these lewd creatures.
The repulsive maidens have been stilled to sleep, those gray
and aged children, they with whom no mortal man,
no god, nor even any beast, will have to do.
It was because of evil they were born, because
they hold the evil darkness of the Pit below
Earth, loathed alike by men and by the heavenly gods.
Nevertheless, run from them, never weaken. They
will track you down as you stride on across the long
land, and your driven feet forever pound the earth,
on across the main water and the circle-washed
cities. Be herdsman to this hard march. Never fail
until you come at last to Pallas' citadel.
Kneel there, and clasp the ancient idol in your arms,
and there we shall find those who will judge this case, and words
to say that will have magic in their figures. Thus
you will be rid of your afflictions, once for all.
For it was I who made you strike your mother down.

Orestes

My lord Apollo, you understand what it means to do
no wrong. Learn also what it is not to neglect.
None can mistrust your power to do good, if you will.

Apollo

Remember: the fear must not give you a beaten heart.
Hermes, you are my brother from a single sire.
Look after him, and as you are named the god who guides,
be such in strong fact. He is my suppliant. Shepherd him
with fortunate escort on his journeys among men.
The wanderer has rights which Zeus acknowledges.

(*Exit Apollo, then Orestes guided by Hermes. Enter the ghost of Clytaemestra.*)

Clytaemestra

You would sleep, then? And what use are you, if you sleep?
It is because of you I go dishonored thus
among the rest of the dead. Because of those I killed
my bad name among the perished suffers no eclipse
but I am driven in disgrace. I say to you
that I am charged with guilt most grave by these. And yet
I suffered too, horribly, and from those most dear,
yet none among the powers is angered for my sake
that I was slaughtered, and by matricidal hands.
Look at these gashes in my heart, think where they came
from. Eyes illuminate the sleeping brain,
but in the daylight man's future cannot be seen.
Yet I have given you much to lap up, outpourings
without wine, sober propitiations, sacrificed
in secrecy of night and on a hearth of fire
for you, at an hour given to no other god.
Now I watch all these honors trampled into the ground,
and he is out and gone away like any fawn
so lightly, from the very middle of your nets,
sprung clear, and laughing merrily at you. Hear me.
It is my life depends upon this spoken plea.
Think then, o goddesses beneath the ground. For I,
the dream of Clytaemestra, call upon your name.

(*The Furies stir in their sleep and whimper.*)

Clytaemestra

Oh, whimper, then, but your man has got away and gone
far. He has friends to help him, who are not like mine.

(*They whimper again.*)

Clytaemestra

Too much sleep and no pity for my plight. I stand,
his mother, here, killed by Orestes. He is gone.

(*They moan in their sleep.*)

Clytaemestra

You moan, you sleep. Get on your feet quickly, will you?
What have you yet got done, except to do evil?

(*They moan again.*)

Clytaemestra

Sleep and fatigue, two masterful conspirators,
have dimmed the deadly anger of the mother-snake.

(*The Chorus start violently, then speak in their sleep.*)

Chorus

Get him, get him, get him, get him. Make sure.

Clytaemestra

The beast you are after is a dream, but like the hound
whose thought of hunting has no lapse, you bay him on.
What are you about? Up, let not work's weariness
beat you, nor slacken with sleep so you forget my pain.
Scold your own heart and hurt it, as it well deserves,
for this is discipline's spur upon her own. Let go
upon this man the stormblasts of your bloodshot breath,
wither him in your wind, after him, hunt him down
once more, and shrivel him in your vitals' heat and flame.

(*The ghost disappears, and the Chorus waken and, as they waken, speak severally.*)

Chorus

Waken. You are awake, wake her, as I did you.
You dream still? On your feet and kick your sleep aside.
Let us see whether this morning-song means vanity.

(*Here they begin to howl.*)

Sisters, we have had wrong done us.
When I have undergone so much and all in vain.
Suffering, suffering, bitter, oh shame shame,
unendurable wrong.
The hunted beast has slipped clean from our nets and gone.
Sleep won me, and I lost my capture.

Shame, son of Zeus! Robber is all you are.
A young god, you have ridden down powers gray with age,
taken the suppliant, though a godless man, who hurt
the mother who gave him birth.
Yourself a god, you stole the matricide away.
Where in this act shall any man say there is right?

The accusation came upon me from my dreams,
and hit me, as with goad in the mid-grip of his fist
the charioteer strikes,
but deep, beneath lobe and heart.
The executioner's cutting whip is mine to feel
and the weight of pain is big, heavy to bear.

Such are the actions of the younger gods. These hold
by unconditional force, beyond all right, a throne
that runs reeking blood,
blood at the feet, blood at the head.
The very stone centre of earth here in our eyes horrible
with blood and curse stands plain to see.

Himself divine, he has spoiled his secret shrine's
hearth with the stain, driven and hallooed the action on.
He made man's way cross the place of the ways of god
and blighted age-old distributions of power.

He has wounded me, but he shall not get this man away.
Let him hide under the ground, he shall never go free.
Cursed suppliant, he shall feel against his head
another murderer rising out of the same seed.

(*Apollo enters again from his sanctuary.*)

Apollo

Get out, I tell you, go and leave this house. Away
in haste, from your presence set the mantic chamber free,
else you may feel the flash and bite of a flying snake
launched from the twisted thong of gold that spans my bow
to make you in your pain spew out the black and foaming
blood of men, vomit the clots sucked from their veins.
This house is no right place for such as you to cling
upon; but where, by judgment given, heads are lopped
and eyes gouged out, throats cut, and by the spoil of sex
the glory of young boys is defeated, where mutilation
lives, and stoning, and the long moan of tortured men
spiked underneath the spine and stuck on pales. Listen
to how the gods spit out the manner of that feast
your loves lean to. The whole cast of your shape is guide
to what you are, the like of whom should hole in the cave
of the blood-reeking lion, not in oracular
interiors, like mine nearby, wipe off your filth.
Out then, you flock of goats without a herdsman, since
no god has such affection as to tend this brood.

Chorus

My lord Apollo, it is your turn to listen now.
Your own part in this is more than accessory.
You are the one who did it; all the guilt is yours.

Apollo

So? How? Continue speaking, until I understand.

Chorus

You gave this outlander the word to kill his mother.

Apollo

The word to exact price for his father. What of that?

Chorus

You then dared take him in, fresh from his bloodletting.

Apollo

Yes, and I told him to take refuge in this house.

Chorus

You are abusive then to those who sped him here?

Apollo

Yes. It was not for you to come near this house;

Chorus

and yet
we have our duty. It was to do what we have done.

Apollo

An office? You? Sound forth your glorious privilege.

Chorus

This: to drive matricides out of their houses.

Apollo

Then
what if it be the woman and she kills her man?

Chorus

Such murder would not be the shedding of kindred blood.

Apollo

You have made into a thing of no account, no place,
the sworn faith of Zeus and of Hera, lady
of consummations, and Cypris by such argument
is thrown away, outlawed, and yet the sweetest things
in man's life come from her, for married love between
man and woman is bigger than oaths, guarded by right
of nature. If when such kill each other you relent
so as not to take vengeance nor eye them in wrath,

then I deny your manhunt of Orestes goes
with right. I see that one cause moves you to strong rage
but on the other clearly you are unmoved to act.
Pallas divine shall review the pleadings of this case.

Chorus

Nothing will ever make me let that man go free.

Apollo

Keep after him then, and make more trouble for yourselves.

Chorus

Do not try to dock my privilege by argument.

Apollo

I would not take your privilege if you gave it me.

Chorus

No, for you are called great beside the throne of Zeus
already, but the motherblood drives me, and I go
to win my right upon this man and hunt him down.

Apollo

But I shall give the suppliant help and rescue, for
if I willingly fail him who turns to me for aid,
his wrath, before gods and men, is a fearful thing.

(They go out, separately. The scene is now Athens, on the Acropolis before the temple and statue of Athene. Orestes enters and takes suppliant posture at the feet of the statue.)

Orestes

My lady Athene, it is at Loxias' behest
I come. Then take in of your grace the wanderer
who comes, no suppliant, not unwashed of hand, but one
blunted at last, and worn and battered on the outland
habitations and the beaten ways of men.
Crossing the dry land and the sea alike, keeping
the ordinances of Apollo's oracle

I come, goddess, before your statue and your house
to keep watch here and wait the issue of my trial.

(The Chorus enter severally, looking for Orestes.)

Chorus

So. Here the man has left a clear trail behind; keep on,
keep on, as the unspeaking accuser tells us, by
whose sense, like hounds after a bleeding fawn, we trail
our quarry by the splash and drip of blood. And now
my lungs are blown with abundant and with wearisome
work, mankilling. My range has been the entire extent
of land, and, flown unwinged across the open water,
I am here, and give way to no ship in my pursuit.
Our man has gone to cover somewhere in this place.
The welcome smell of human blood has told me so.

Look again, look again,
search everywhere, let
not the matricide
steal away and escape.

(They see Orestes.)

See there! He clings to defence
again, his arms winding the immortal goddess'
image, so tries to be quit out of our hands.
It shall not be. His mother's blood spilled on the ground
can not come back again.
It is all soaked and drained into the ground and gone.

You must give back for her blood from the living man
red blood of your body to suck, and from your own
I could feed, with bitter-swallowed drench,
turn your strength limp while yet you live and drag you down
where you must pay for the pain of the murdered mother,
and watch the rest of the mortals stained with violence
against god or guest
or hurt parents who were close and dear,
each with the pain upon him that his crime deserves.
Hades is great, Hades calls men to reckoning

there under the ground,
sees all, and cuts it deep in his recording mind.

Orestes

I have been beaten and been taught, I understand
the many rules of absolution, where it is right
to speak and where be silent. In this action now
speech has been ordered by my teacher, who is wise.
The stain of blood dulls now and fades upon my hand.
My blot of matricide is being washed away.
When it was fresh still, at the hearth of the god, Phoebus,
this was absolved and driven out by sacrifice
of swine, and the list were long if I went back to tell
of all I met who were not hurt by being with me.
Time in his aging overtakes all things alike.
Now it is from pure mouth and with good auspices
I call upon Athene, queen of this land, to come
and rescue me. She, without work of her spear, shall win
myself and all my land and all the Argive host
to stand her staunch companion for the rest of time.
Whether now ranging somewhere in the Libyan land
beside her father's crossing and by Triton's run
of waters she sets upright or enshrouded foot
rescuing there her friends, or on the Phlegraean flat
like some bold man of armies sweeps with eyes the scene,
let her come! She is a god and hears me far away.
So may she set me free from what is at my back.

Chorus

Neither Apollo nor Athene's strength must win
you free, save you from going down forgotten, without
knowing where joy lies anywhere inside your heart,
blood drained, chewed dry by the powers of death, a wraith, a
shell.
You will not speak to answer, spew my challenge away?
You are consecrate to me and fattened for my feast,

and you shall feed me while you live, not cut down first
at the altar. Hear the spell I sing to bind you in.

Come then, link we our choral. Ours
to show forth the power
and terror of our music, declare
our rights of office, how we conspire
to steer men's lives.
We hold we are straight and just. If a man
can spread his hands and show they are clean,
no wrath of ours shall lurk for him.
Unscathed he walks through his life time.
But one like this man before us, with stained
hidden hands, and the guilt upon him,
shall find us beside him, as witnesses
of the truth, and we show clear in the end
to avenge the blood of the murdered.

Mother, o my mother night, who gave me
birth, to be a vengeance on the seeing
and the blind, hear me. For Leto's
youngling takes my right away,
stealing from my clutch the prey
that crouches, whose blood would wipe
at last the motherblood away.

Over the beast doomed to the fire
this is the chant, scatter of wits,
frenzy and fear, hurting the heart,
song of the Furies
binding brain and blighting blood
in its stringless melody.

This the purpose that the all-involving
destiny spun, to be ours and to be shaken
never: when mortals assume outrage
of own hand in violence,
these we dog, till one goes

under earth. Nor does death
set them altogether free.

Over the beast doomed to the fire
this is the chant, scatter of wits,
frenzy and fear, hurting the heart,
song of the Furies
binding brain and blighting blood
in its stringless melody.

When we were born such lots were assigned for our keeping.
So the immortals must hold hands off, nor is there
one who shall sit at our feasting.
For sheer white robes I have no right and no portion.

I have chosen overthrow
of houses, where the Battlegod
grown within strikes near and dear
down. So we swoop upon this man
here. He is strong, but we wear him down
for the blood that is still wet on him.

Here we stand in our haste to wrench from all others
these devisings, make the gods clear of our counsels
so that even appeal comes
not to them, since Zeus has ruled our blood dripping company
outcast, nor will deal with us.

I have chosen overthrow
of houses, where the Battlegod
grown within strikes near and dear
down. So we swoop upon this man
here. He is strong, but we wear him down
for the blood that is still wet on him.

Men's illusions in their pride under the sky melt
down, and are diminished into the ground, gone
before the onset of our black robes, pulsing
of our vindictive feet against them.

For with a long leap from high
above and dead drop of weight
I bring foot's force crashing down
to cut the legs from under even
the runner, and spill him to ruin.

He falls, and does not know in the daze of his folly.
Such in the dark of man is the mist of infection
that hovers, and moaning rumor tells how his house lies
under fog that glooms above.

For with a long leap from high
above, and dead drop of weight,
I bring foot's force crashing down
to cut the legs from under even
the runner, and spill him to ruin.

All holds. For we are strong and skilled;
we have authority; we hold
memory of evil; we are stern
nor can men's pleadings bend us. We
drive through our duties, spurned, outcast
from gods, driven apart to stand in light
not of the sun. So sheer with rock are ways
for those who see, as upon those whose eyes are lost.

Is there a man who does not fear
this, does not shrink to hear
how my place has been ordained,
granted and given by destiny
and god, absolute? Privilege
primeval yet is mine, nor am I without place
though it be underneath the ground
and in no sunlight and in gloom that I must stand.

(Athene enters, in full armor.)

Athene

From far away I heard the outcry of your call.
It was beside Scamandrus. I was taking seisin
of land, for there the Achaean lords of war and first

fighters gave me large portion of all their spears
had won, the land root and stock to be mine for all
eternity, for the sons of Theseus a choice gift.
From there, sped on my weariless feet, I came, wingless
but in the rush and speed of the aegis fold. And now
I see upon this land a novel company
which, though it brings no terror to my eyes, brings still
wonder. Who are you? I address you all alike,
both you, the stranger kneeling at my image here,
and you, who are like no seed ever begotten, not
seen ever by the gods as goddesses, nor yet
stamped in the likenesses of any human form.
But no. This is the place of the just. Its rights forbid
even the innocent to speak evil of his mates.

Chorus

Daughter of Zeus, you shall hear all compressed to brief
measure. We are the gloomy children of the night.
Curses they call us in our homes beneath the ground.

Athene

I know your race, then, and the names by which you are called.

Chorus

You shall be told of our position presently.

Athene

I can know that, if one will give me a clear account.

Chorus

We drive from home those who have shed the blood of men.

Athene

Where is the place, then, where the killer's flight shall end?

Chorus

A place where happiness is nevermore allowed.

Athene

Is he one? Do you blast him to this kind of flight?

Chorus

Yes. He murdered his mother by deliberate choice.

Athene

By random force, or was it fear of someone's wrath?

Chorus

Where is the spur to justify man's matricide?

Athene

Here are two sides, and only half the argument.

Chorus

He is unwilling to give or to accept an oath.

Athene

You wish to be called righteous rather than act right.

Chorus

No. How so? Out of the riches of your wit, explain.

Athene

I say, wrong must not win by technicalities.

Chorus

Examine him then yourself. Decide it, and be fair.

Athene

You would turn over authority in this case to me?

Chorus

By all means. Your father's degree, and yours, deserve as much.

Athene

Your turn, stranger. What will you say in answer? Speak,
tell me your country and your birth, what has befallen
you, then defend yourself against the anger of these;
if it was confidence in the right that made you sit
to keep this image near my hearth, a supplicant
in the tradition of Ixion, sacrosanct.
Give me an answer which is plain to understand.

Orestes

Lady Athene, first I will take the difficult thought
away that lies in these last words you spoke. I am
no supplicant, nor was it because I had a stain
upon my hand that I sat at your image. I
will give you a strong proof that what I say is true.
It is the law that the man of the bloody hand must speak
no word until, by action of one who can cleanse,
blood from a young victim has washed his blood away.
Long since, at the homes of others, I have been absolved
thus, both by running waters and by victims slain.

I count this scruple now out of the way. Learn next
with no delay where I am from. I am of Argos
and it is to my honor that you ask the name
of my father, Agamemnon, lord of seafarers,
and your companion when you made the Trojan city
of Ilium no city any more. He died
without honor when he came home. It was my mother
of the dark heart, who entangled him in subtle gyves
and cut him down. The bath is witness to his death.
I was an exile in the time before this. I came back
and killed the woman who gave me birth. I plead guilty.
My father was dear, and this was vengeance for his blood.
Apollo shares responsibility for this.
He counterspurred my heart and told me of pains to come
if I should fail to act against the guilty ones.
This is my case. Decide if it be right or wrong.
I am in your hands. Where my fate falls, I shall accept.

Athene

The matter is too big for any mortal man
who thinks he can judge it. Even I have not the right
to analyse cases of murder where wrath's edge
is sharp, and all the more since you have come, and clung
a clean and innocent supplicant, against my doors.
You bring no harm to my city. I respect your rights.

Yet these, too, have their work. We cannot brush them aside,
and if this action so runs that they fail to win,
the venom of their resolution will return
to infect the soil, and sicken all my land to death.
Here is dilemma. Whether I let them stay or drive
them off, it is a hard course and will hurt. Then, since
the burden of the case is here, and rests on me,
I shall select judges of manslaughter, and swear
them in, establish a court into all time to come.

Litigants, call your witnesses, have ready your proofs
as evidence under bond to keep this case secure.
I will pick the finest of my citizens, and come
back. They shall swear to make no judgment that is not
just, and make clear where in this action the truth lies.

(*Exit.*)

Chorus

Here is overthrow of all
the young laws, if the claim
of this matricide shall stand
good, his crime be sustained.
Should this be, every man will find a way
to act at his own caprice;
over and over again in time
to come, parents shall await
the deathstroke at their children's hands.

We are the Angry Ones. But we
shall watch no more over works
of men, and so act. We shall
let loose indiscriminate death.
Man shall learn from man's lot, forejudge
the evils of his neighbor's case,
see respite and windfall in storm:
pathetic prophet who consoles
with strengthless cures, in vain.

Nevermore let one who feels
the stroke of accident, uplift
his voice and make outcry, thus:
"Oh Justice!
Throned powers of the Furies, help!"
Such might be the pitiful cry
of some father, of the stricken
mother, their appeal. Now
the House of Justice has collapsed.

There are times when fear is good.
It must keep its watchful place
at the heart's controls. There is
advantage
in the wisdom won from pain.
Should the city, should the man
rear a heart that nowhere goes
in fear, how shall such a one
any more respect the right?

Refuse the life of anarchy;
refuse the life devoted to
one master.
The in-between has the power
by God's grant always, though
his ordinances vary.
I will speak in defence
of reason: for the very child
of vanity is violence;
but out of health
in the heart issues the beloved
and the longed-for, prosperity.

All for all I say to you:
bow before the altar of right.
You shall not
eye advantage, and heel
it over with foot of force.

Vengeance will be upon you.
The all is bigger than you.
Let man see this and take
care, to mother and father,
and to the guest
in the gates welcomed, give all rights
that befall their position.

The man who does right, free-willed, without constraint
shall not lose happiness
nor be wiped out with all his generation.
But the transgressor, I tell you, the bold man
who brings in confusion of goods unrightly won,
at long last and perforce, when ship toils
under tempest must strike his sail
in the wreck of his rigging.

He calls on those who hear not, caught inside
the hard wrestle of water.
The spirit laughs at the hot hearted man,
the man who said "never to me," watches him
pinned in distress, unable to run free of the crests.
He had good luck in his life. Now
he smashes it on the reef of Right
and drowns, unwept and forgotten.

(*Athene re-enters, guiding twelve citizens chosen as jurors and attended by a herald. Other citizens follow.*)

Athene

Herald, make proclamation and hold in the host
assembled. Let the stabbing voice of the Etruscan
trumpet, blown to the full with mortal wind, crash out
its high call to all the assembled populace
For in the filling of this senatorial ground
it is best for all the city to be silent and learn
the measures I have laid down into the rest of time.
So too these litigants, that their case be fairly tried.

(*Trumpet call. All take their places. Enter Apollo.*)

Chorus

My lord Apollo, rule within your own domain.
What in this matter has to do with you? Declare.

Apollo

I come to testify. This man, by observed law,
came to me as suppliant, took his place by hearth and hall,
and it was I who cleaned him of the stain of blood.
I have also come to help him win his case. I bear
responsibility for his mother's murder.

(*To Athene.*)

You
who know the rules, initiate the trial. Preside.

Athene (to the Furies)

I declare the trial opened. Yours is the first word.
For it must justly be the pursuer who speaks first
and opens the case, and makes plain what the action is.

Chorus

We are many, but we shall cut it short. You, then,
word against word answer our charges one by one.
Say first, did you kill your mother or did you not?

Orestes

Yes, I killed her. There shall be no denial of that.

Chorus

There are three falls in the match and one has gone to us.

Orestes

So you say. But you have not even thrown your man.

Chorus

So. Then how did you kill her? You are bound to say.

Orestes

I do. With drawn sword in my hand I cut her throat.

Chorus

By whose persuasion and advice did you do this?

Orestes

By order of this god, here. So he testifies.

Chorus

The Prophet guided you into this matricide?

Orestes

Yes. I have never complained of this. I do not now.

Chorus

When sentence seizes you, you will talk a different way.

Orestes

I have no fear. My father will aid me from the grave.

Chorus

Kill your mother, then put trust in a corpse! Trust on.

Orestes

Yes. She was dirtied twice over with disgrace.

Chorus

Tell me how, and explain it to the judges here.

Orestes

She murdered her husband, and thereby my father too.

Chorus

Of this stain, death has set her free. But you still live.

Orestes

When she lived, why did you not descend and drive her out?

Chorus

The man she killed was not of blood congenital.

Orestes

But am I then involved with my mother by blood-bond?

Chorus

Murderer, yes. How else could she have nursed you beneath
her heart? Do you forswear your mother's intimate blood?

Orestes

Yours to bear witness now, Apollo, and expound
the case for me, if I was right to cut her down.
I will not deny I did this thing, because I did
do it. But was the bloodshed right or not? Decide
and answer. As you answer, I shall state my case.

Apollo

To you, established by Athene in your power,
I shall speak justly. I am a prophet, I shall not
lie. Never, for man, woman, nor city, from my throne
of prophecy have I spoken a word, except
that which Zeus, father of Olympians, might command.
This is justice. Recognize then how great its strength.
I tell you, follow our father's will. For not even
the oath that binds you is more strong than Zeus is strong.

Chorus

Then Zeus, as you say, authorized the oracle
to this Orestes, stating he could wreak the death
of his father on his mother, and it would have no force?

Apollo

It is not the same thing for a man of blood to die
honored with the king's staff given by the hand of god,
and that by means of a woman, not with the far cast
of fierce arrows, as an Amazon might have done,
but in a way that you shall hear, o Pallas and you
who sit in state to judge this action by your vote.

He had come home from his campaigning. He had done
better than worse, in the eyes of a fair judge. She lay
in wait for him. It was the bath. When he was at
its edge, she hooded the robe on him, and in the blind
and complex toils tangled her man, and chopped him down.

There is the story of the death of a great man,
solemn in all men's sight, lord of the host of ships.

I have called the woman what she was, so that the people
whose duty it is to try this case may be inflamed.

Chorus

Zeus, by your story, gives first place to the father's death.
Yet Zeus himself shackled elder Cronus, his own
father. Is this not contradiction? I testify,
judges, that this is being said in your hearing.

Apollo

You foul animals, from whom the gods turn in disgust,
Zeus could undo shackles, such hurt can be made good,
and there is every kind of way to get out. But once
the dust has drained down all a man's blood, once the man
has died, there is no raising of him up again.
This is a thing for which my father never made
curative spells. All other states, without effort
of hard breath, he can completely rearrange.

Chorus

See what it means to force acquittal of this man.
He has spilled his mother's blood upon the ground. Shall he
then be at home in Argos in his father's house?
What altars of the community shall he use? Is there
a brotherhood's lustration that will let him in?

Apollo

I will tell you, and I will answer correctly. Watch.
The mother is no parent of that which is called
her child, but only nurse of the new-planted seed
that grows. The parent is he who mounts. A stranger she
preserves a stranger's seed, if no god interfere.
I will show you proof of what I have explained. There can
be a father without any mother. There she stands,
the living witness, daughter of Olympian Zeus,
she who was never fostered in the dark of the womb
yet such a child as no goddess could bring to birth.
In all else, Pallas, as I best may understand,

I shall make great your city and its populace.
So I have brought this man to sit beside the hearth
of your house, to be your true friend for the rest of time,
so you shall win him, goddess, to fight by your side,
and among men to come this shall stand a strong bond
that his and your own people's children shall be friends.

Athene

Shall I assume that enough has now been said, and tell
the judges to render what they believe a true verdict?

Chorus

Every arrow we had has been shot now. We wait
on their decision, to see how the case has gone.

Athene

So then. How shall I act correctly in your eyes?

Apollo

You have heard what you have heard, and as you cast your votes,
good friends, respect in your hearts the oath that you have sworn.

Athene

If it please you, men of Attica, hear my decree
now, on this first case of bloodletting I have judged.
For Aegeus' population, this forevermore
shall be the ground where justices deliberate.
Here is the Hill of Ares, here the Amazons
encamped and built their shelters when they came in arms
for spite of Theseus, here they piled their rival towers
to rise, new city, and dare his city long ago,
and slew their beasts for Ares. So this rock is named
from then the Hill of Ares. Here the reverence
of citizens, their fear and kindred do-no-wrong
shall hold by day and in the blessing of night alike
all while the people do not muddy their own laws
with foul infusions. But if bright water you stain
with mud, you nevermore will find it fit to drink.

No anarchy, no rule of a single master. Thus
I advise my citizens to govern and to grace,
and not to cast fear utterly from your city. What
man who fears nothing at all is ever righteous? Such
be your just terrors, and you may deserve and have
salvation for your citadel, your land's defence,
such as is nowhere else found among men, neither
among the Scythians, nor the land that Pelops held.
I establish this tribunal. It shall be untouched
by money-making, grave but quick to wrath, watchful
to protect those who sleep, a sentry on the land.

These words I have unreeled are for my citizens,
advice into the future. All must stand upright
now, take each man his ballot in his hand, think on
his oath, and make his judgment. For my word is said.

Chorus

I give you counsel by no means to disregard
this company. We can be a weight to crush your land.

Apollo

I speak too. I command you to fear, and not
make void the yield of oracles from Zeus and me.

Chorus

You honor bloody actions where you have no right.
The oracles you give shall be no longer clean.

Apollo

My father's purposes are twisted then. For he
was appealed to by Ixion, the first murderer.

Chorus

Talk! But for my part, if I do not win the case,
I shall come back to this land and it will feel my weight.

Apollo

Neither among the elder nor the younger gods
have you consideration. I shall win this suit.

Chorus

Such was your action in the house of Pheres. Then
you beguiled the Fates to let mortals go free from death.

Apollo

Is it not right to do well by the man who shows
you worship, and above all when he stands in need?

Chorus

You won the ancient goddesses over with wine
and so destroyed the orders of an elder time.

Apollo

You shall not win the issue of this suit, but shall
be made to void your poison to no enemy's hurt.

Chorus

Since you, a young god, would ride down my elder age,
I must stay here and listen to how the trial goes,
being yet uncertain to loose my anger on the state.

Athene

It is my task to render final judgment here.
This is a ballot for Orestes I shall cast.
There is no mother anywhere who gave me birth,
and, but for marriage, I am always for the male
with all my heart, and strongly on my father's side.
So, in a case where the wife has killed her husband, lord
of the house, her death shall not mean most to me. And if
the other votes are even, then Orestes wins.
You of the jurymen who have this duty assigned,
shake out the ballots from the vessels, with all speed.

Orestes

Phoebus Apollo, what will the decision be?

Chorus

Darkness of night, our mother, are you here to watch?

Orestes

This is the end for me. The noose, or else the light.

Chorus

Here our destruction, or our high duties confirmed.

Apollo

Shake out the votes accurately, Athenian friends.
Be careful as you pick them up. Make no mistake.
In the lapse of judgment great disaster comes. The cast
of a single ballot has restored a house entire.

Athene

The man before us has escaped the charge of blood.
The ballots are in equal number for each side.

Orestes

Pallas Athene, you have kept my house alive.
When I had lost the land of my fathers you gave me
a place to live. Among the Hellenes they shall say:
"A man of Argos lives again in the estates
of his father, all by grace of Pallas Athene, and
Apollo, and with them the all-ordaining god
the Savior"—who remembers my father's death, who looked
upon my mother's advocates, and rescues me.
I shall go home now, but before I go I swear
to this your country and to this your multitude
of people into all the bigness of time to be,
that never man who holds the helm of my state shall come
against your country in the ordered strength of spears,
but though I lie then in my grave, I still shall wreak
helpless bad luck and misadventure upon all
who stride across the oath that I have sworn: their ways
disconsolate make, their crossings full of evil
augury, so they shall be sorry that they moved.
But while they keep the upright way, and hold in high
regard the city of Pallas, and align their spears
to fight beside her, I shall be their gracious spirit.

And so farewell, you and your city's populace.
May you outwrestle and overthrow all those who come
against you, to your safety and your spears' success.

(Exit. Exit also Apollo.)

Chorus

Gods of the younger generation, you have ridden down
the laws of the elder time, torn them out of my hands.
I, disinherited, suffering, heavy with anger
shall let loose on the land
the vindictive poison
dripping deadly out of my heart upon the ground;
this from itself shall breed
cancer, the leafless, the barren
to strike, for the right, their low lands
and drag its smear of mortal infection on the ground.
What shall I do? Afflicted
I am mocked by these people.
I have borne what can not
be borne. Great the sorrows and the dishonor upon
the sad daughters of night.

Athene

Listen to me. I would not have you be so grieved.
For you have not been beaten. This was the result
of a fair ballot which was even. You were not
dishonored, but the luminous evidence of Zeus
was there, and he who spoke the oracle was he
who ordered Orestes so to act and not be hurt.
Do not be angry any longer with this land
nor bring the bulk of your hatred down on it, do not
render it barren of fruit, nor spill the dripping rain
of death in fierce and jagged lines to eat the seeds.
In complete honesty I promise you a place
of your own, deep hidden under ground that is yours by right
where you shall sit on shining chairs beside the hearth
to accept devotions offered by your citizens.

Chorus

Gods of the younger generation, you have ridden down
the laws of the elder time, torn them out of my hands.
I, disinherited, suffering, heavy with anger
shall let loose on the land
the vindictive poison
dripping deadly out of my heart upon the ground;
this from itself shall breed
cancer, the leafless, the barren
to strike, for the right, their low lands
and drag its smear of mortal infection on the ground.
What shall I do? Afflicted
I am mocked by these people.
I have borne what can not
be borne. Great the sorrow and the dishonor upon
the sad daughters of night.

Athene

No, not dishonored. You are goddesses. Do not
in too much anger make this place of mortal men
uninhabitable. I have Zeus behind me. Do
we need to speak of that? I am the only god
who know the keys to where his thunderbolts are locked.
We do not need such, do we? Be reasonable
and do not from a reckless mouth cast on the land
spells that will ruin every thing which might bear fruit.
No. Put to sleep the bitter strength in the black wave
and live with me and share my pride of worship. Here
is a big land, and from it you shall win first fruits
in offerings for children and the marriage rite
for always. Then you will say my argument was good.

Chorus

That they could treat me so!
I, the mind of the past, to be driven under the ground
out cast, like dirt!
The wind I breathe is fury and utter hate.

Earth, ah, earth
what is this agony that crawls under my ribs?
Night, hear me, o Night,
mother. They have wiped me out
and the hard hands of the gods
and their treacheries have taken my old rights away.

Athene

I will bear your angers. You are elder born than I
and in that you are wiser far than I. Yet still
Zeus gave me too intelligence not to be despised.
If you go away into some land of foreigners,
I warn you, you will come to love this country. Time
in his forward flood shall ever grow more dignified
for the people of this city. And you, in your place
of eminence beside Erechtheus in his house
shall win from female and from male processionals
more than all lands of men beside could ever give.
Only in this place that I haunt do not inflict
your bloody stimulus to twist the inward hearts
of young men, raging in a fury not of wine,
nor, as if plucking the heart from fighting cocks,
engraft among my citizens that spirit of war
that turns their battle fury inward on themselves.
No, let our wars range outward hard against the man
who has fallen horribly in love with high renown.
No true fighter I call the bird that fights at home.
Such life I offer you, and it is yours to take.
Do good, receive good, and be honored as the good
are honored. Share our country, the beloved of god.

Chorus

That they could treat me so!
I, the mind of the past, to be driven under the ground
out cast, like dirt!
The wind I breathe is fury and utter hate.
Earth, ah, earth

what is this agony that crawls under my ribs?
Night, hear me, o Night,
mother. They have wiped me out
and the hard hands of the gods
and their treacheries have taken my old rights away.

Athene

I will not weary of telling you all the good things
I offer, so that you can never say that you,
an elder god, were driven unfriended from the land
by me in my youth, and by my mortal citizens.
But if you hold Persuasion has her sacred place
of worship, in the sweet beguilement of my voice,
then you might stay with us. But if you wish to stay
then it would not be justice to inflict your rage
upon this city, your resentment or bad luck
to armies. Yours the baron's portion in this land
if you will, in all justice, with full privilege.

Chorus

Lady Athene, what is this place you say is mine?

Athene

A place free of all grief and pain. Take it for yours.

Chorus

If I do take it, shall I have some definite powers?

Athene

No household shall be prosperous without your will.

Chorus

You will do this? You will really let me be so strong?

Athene

So we shall straighten the lives of all who worship us.

Chorus

You guarantee such honor for the rest of time?

Athene

I have no need to promise what I can not do.

Chorus

I think you will have your way with me. My hate is going.

Athene

Stay here, then. You will win the hearts of others, too.

Chorus

I will put a spell upon the land. What shall it be?

Athene

Something that has no traffic with evil success.
Let it come out of the ground, out of the sea's water,
and from the high air make the waft of gentle gales
wash over the country in full sunlight, and the seed
and stream of the soil's yield and of the grazing beasts
be strong and never fail our people as time goes,
and make the human seed be kept alive. Make more
the issue of those who worship more your ways, for as
the gardener works in love, so love I best of all
the unblighted generation of these upright men.
All such is yours for granting. In the speech and show
and pride of battle, I myself shall not endure
this city's eclipse in the estimation of mankind.

Chorus

I accept this home at Athene's side.
I shall not forget the cause
of this city, which Zeus all powerful and Ares
rule, stronghold of divinities,
glory of Hellene gods, their guarded altar.
So with forecast of good
I speak this prayer for them
that the sun's bright magnificence shall break out wave
on wave of all the happiness
life can give, across their land

Athene

Here are my actions. In all good will
toward these citizens I establish in power
spirits who are large, difficult to soften.
To them is given the handling entire
of men's lives. That man
who has not felt the weight of their hands
takes the strokes of life, knows not whence, not why,
for crimes wreaked in past generations
drag him before these powers. Loud his voice
but the silent doom
hates hard, and breaks him to dust.

Chorus

Let there blow no wind that wrecks the trees.
I pronounce words of grace.
Nor blaze of heat blind the blossoms of grown plants, nor
cross the circles of its right
place. Let no barren deadly sickness creep and kill.
Flocks fatten. Earth be kind
to them, with double fold of fruit
in time appointed for its yielding. Secret child
of earth, her hidden wealth, bestow
blessing and surprise of gods.

Athene

Strong guard of our city, hear you these
and what they portend? Fury is a high queen
of strength even among the immortal gods
and the undergods, and for humankind
their work is accomplished, absolute, clear:
for some, singing; for some, life dimmed
in tears; theirs the disposition.

Chorus

Death of manhood cut down
before its prime I forbid:

girls' grace and glory find
men to live life with them.
Grant, you who have the power.
And o, steering spirits of law,
goddesses of destiny,
sisters from my mother, hear;
in all houses implicate,
in all time heavy of hand
on whom your just arrest befalls,
august among goddesses, bestow.

Athene

It is my glory to hear how these
generosities
are given my land. I admire the eyes
of Persuasion, who guided the speech of my mouth
toward these, when they were reluctant and wild.
Zeus, who guides men's speech in councils, was too
strong; and my ambition
for good wins out in the whole issue.

Chorus

This my prayer: Civil War
fattening on men's ruin shall
not thunder in our city. Let
not the dry dust that drinks
the black blood of citizens
through passion for revenge
and bloodshed for bloodshed
be given our state to prey upon.
Let them render grace for grace.
Let love be their common will;
let them hate with single heart.
Much wrong in the world thereby is healed.

Athene

Are they taking thought to discover that road
where speech goes straight?

In the terror upon the faces of these
I see great good for our citizens.
While with good will you hold in high honor
these spirits, their will shall be good, as you steer
your city, your land
on an upright course clear through to the end.

Chorus

Farewell, farewell. High destiny shall be yours
by right. Farewell, citizens
seated near the throne of Zeus,
beloved by the maiden he loves,
civilized as years go by,
sheltered under Athene's wings,
grand even in her father's sight.

Athene

Goddesses, farewell. Mine to lead, as these
attend us, to where
by the sacred light new chambers are given.
Go then. Sped by majestic sacrifice
from these, plunge beneath the ground. There hold
off what might hurt the land; pour in
the city's advantage, success in the end.
You, children of Cranaus, you who keep
the citadel, guide these guests of the state.
For good things given,
your hearts' desire be for good to return.

Chorus

Farewell and again farewell, words spoken twice over,
all who by this citadel,
mortal men, spirits divine,
hold the city of Pallas, grace
this my guestship in your land.
Life will give you no regrets.

Athene

Well said. I assent to all the burden of your prayers,
and by the light of flaring torches now attend
your passage to the deep and subterranean hold,
as by us walk those women whose high privilege
it is to guard my image. Flower of all the land
of Theseus, let them issue now, grave companies,
maidens, wives, elder women, in processional.
In the investiture of purple stained robes
dignify them, and let the torchlight go before
so that the kindly company of these within
our ground may shine in the future of strong men to come.

Chorus (by the women who have been forming for processional)

Home, home, o high, o aspiring
Daughters of Night, aged children, in blithe processional.
Bless them, all here, with silence.

In the primeval dark of earth-hollows
held in high veneration with rights sacrificial
bless them, all people, with silence.

Gracious be, wish what the land wishes,
follow, grave goddesses, flushed in the flamesprung
torchlight gay on your journey.
Singing all follow our footsteps.

There shall be peace forever between these people
of Pallas and their guests. Zeus the all seeing
met with Destiny to confirm it.
Singing all follow our footsteps.

(*Exeunt omnes, in procession.*)

PHILOCTETES

Translated by David Grene

INTRODUCTION

Philoctetes was produced in 409 B.C., when Sophocles was nearly eighty, and won first prize.

Philoctetes was the lawful master of the great bow of Heracles. He joined the Achaean expedition against Troy but, in guiding his mates to a place of sacrifice, he was bitten in the foot by a snake, and the wound would not heal. Because of the stench of the festering sore and the man's inauspicious cries, he was marooned on Lemnos. But after the death of Achilles, the Greeks found from prophecies that they could not take Troy without Philoctetes and his bow, and had to send an embassy to beg or beguile him to come back. Restored and healed at last, he played the leading part in the final battles at Troy. The story is told in the epic continuations of Homer, barely noticed, though obviously known, by Homer himself. It is an excellent theme for tragedy, being an example of a plot fully tragic in the Greek, though perhaps not in the modern, sense, which yet has a necessarily happy ending. Many plays called *Philoctetes* are recorded, but all except the one by Sophocles are lost. Aeschylus produced one, of unknown date, and so did Euripides, along with *Medea* in 431 B.C.

The circumstances of the wound and the plight of Philoctetes, the identity of the hero or heroes assigned to reclaim him, the means used—these vary in the tradition. Here, to Odysseus, the intelligent, persistent, ruthless spirit of the Greek war against Troy, Sophocles has added as collaborator the young Neoptolemus, son of Achilles and pre-eminent fighting man, who, schooled by Odysseus, wins the bow from Philoctetes. But he acts against his nature in so doing. Caught between military duty and his personal integrity, he must, as a Sophoclean hero, follow the dictates of the latter. At the end, he is ready to give up his career of glory and the cause of the Trojan War, and only the command of the deified Heracles saves the situation.

Philoctetes is a drama of the adventures of characters, reduced to its simplest terms. All three main persons are drawn with convincing care. The chorus is minimal, the lyrics reduced in scope. There is almost no decoration. This comes close to being prose drama, in which the poetry comes unobtrusively, chiefly from Philoctetes' deep love for inanimate or inhuman things—his bow, his wilderness household, and the spirits of the wild place which would have destroyed him but which he has mastered in his lonely struggle for survival.

CHARACTERS

Odysseus

Chorus of Sailors under the Command of Neoptolemus

The Spy Disguised as a Trader

Neoptolemus, Prince of Scyrus and Son of Achilles

Philoctetes

Heracles

PHILOCTETES

SCENE: *A lonely spot on the island of Lemnos. Enter Odysseus and Neoptolemus.*

Odysseus

This is it; this Lemnos and its beach
down to the sea that quite surrounds it; desolate,
no one sets foot on it; there are no houses.
This is where I marooned him long ago,
the son of Poias, the Melian, his foot
diseased and eaten away with running ulcers.

Son of our greatest hero,
son of Achilles, Neoptolemus,
I tell you I had orders for what I did:
my masters, the princes, bade me do it.

We had no peace with him: at the holy festivals,
we dared not touch the wine and meat; he screamed
and groaned so, and those terrible cries of his
brought ill luck on our celebrations; all
the camp was haunted by him.

Now is no time to talk to you of this,
now is no time for long speeches.
I am afraid that he may hear of my coming
and ruin all my plans to take him.

It is you who must help me with the rest. Look about
and see where there might be a cave with two mouths.
There are two niches to rest in, one in the sun
when it is cold, the other a tunneled passage
through which the breezes blow in summertime.

A man can sleep there and be cool. To the left,
a little, you may see a spring to drink at—
if it is still unchoked—go this way quietly,
see if he's there or somewhere else and signal.
Then I can tell you the rest. Listen:
I shall tell you. We will both do this thing.

Neoptolemus

What you speak of is near at hand, Odysseus.
I think I see such a cave.

Odysseus

Above or below? I cannot see it myself.

Neoptolemus

Above here, and no trace of a footpath.

Odysseus

See if he is housed within, asleep.

Neoptolemus

I see an empty hut, with no one there.

Odysseus

And nothing to keep house with?

Neoptolemus

A pallet bed, stuffed with leaves, to sleep on, for someone.

Odysseus

And nothing else? Nothing inside the house?

Neoptolemus

A cup, made of a single block, a poor
workman's contrivance. And some kindling, too.

Odysseus

It is his treasure house that you describe.

Neoptolemus

And look, some rags are drying in the sun
full of the oozing matter from a sore.

Odysseus

Yes, certainly he lives here, even now
is somewhere not far off. He cannot go far,
sick as he is, lame cripple for so long.
It's likely he has gone to search for food
or somewhere that he knows there is a herb
to ease his pain. Send your man here to watch,
that he may not come upon me without warning.
For he would rather take me than all the Greeks.

Neoptolemus

Very well, then, the path will be watched.
Go on with your story; tell me what you want.

Odysseus

Son of Achilles,
our coming here has a purpose; to it be loyal
with more than with your body. If you should hear
some strange new thing, unlike what you have heard
before, still serve us; it was to serve you came here.

Neoptolemus

What would you have me do?

Odysseus

Ensnare
the soul of Philoctetes with your words.
When he asks who you are and whence you came,
say you are Achilles' son; you need not lie.
Say you are sailing home, leaving the Greeks
and all their fleet, in bitter hatred. Say
that they had prayed you, urged you from your home,
and swore that only with your help
could Troy be taken. Yet when you came and asked,
as by your right, to have your father's arms,
Achilles' arms, they did not think you worthy
but gave them to Odysseus. Say what you will
against me; do not spare me anything.

Nothing of this will hurt me; if you will not
do this, you will bring sorrow on all the Greeks.
If this man's bow shall not be taken by us,
you cannot sack the town of Troy.

Perhaps you wonder why you can safely meet him,
why he would trust you and not me. Let me explain.
You have come here unforced, unpledged by oaths,
made no part of our earlier expedition.
The opposite is true in my own case;
at no point can I deny his charge.
If, when he sees me, Philoctetes
still has his bow, there is an end of me,
and you too, for my company would damn you.
For this you must sharpen your wits, to become a thief
of the arms no man has conquered.

I know, young man, it is not your natural bent
to say such things nor to contrive such mischief.
But the prize of victory is pleasant to win.
Bear up: another time we shall prove honest.
For one brief shameless portion of a day
give me yourself, and then for all the rest
you may be called most scrupulous of men.

Neoptolemus

Son of Laertes, what I dislike to hear
I hate to put in execution.
I have a natural antipathy
to get my ends by tricks and stratagems.
So, too, they say, my father was. Philoctetes
I will gladly fight and capture, bring him with us,
but not by treachery. Surely a one-legged man
cannot prevail against so many of us!
I recognize that I was sent with you
to follow your instructions. I am loath
to have you call me traitor. Still, my lord,

I would prefer even to fail with honor
than win by cheating.

Odysseus

You are a good man's son.
I was young, too, once, and then I had a tongue
very inactive and a doing hand.
Now as I go forth to the test, I see
that everywhere among the race of men
it is the tongue that wins and not the deed.

Neoptolemus

What do you bid me do, but to tell lies?

Odysseus

By craft I bid you take him, Philoctetes.

Neoptolemus

And why by craft rather than by persuasion?

Odysseus

He will not be persuaded; force will fail.

Neoptolemus

Has he such strength to give him confidence?

Odysseus

The arrows none may avoid, that carry death.

Neoptolemus

Then even to encounter him is not safe?

Odysseus

Not if you do not take him by craft, as I told you.

Neoptolemus

Do you not find it vile yourself, this lying?

Osysseus

Not if the lying brings our rescue with it.

Neoptolemus

How can a man not blush to say such things?

Odysseus
When one does something for gain, one need not blush.

Neoptolemus
What gain for me that he should come to Troy?

Odysseus
His weapons alone are destined to take Troy.

Neoptolemus
Then I shall not be, as was said, its conqueror?

Odysseus
Not you apart from them nor they from you.

Neoptolemus
They must be my quarry then, if this is so.

Odysseus
You will win a double prize if you do this.

Neoptolemus
What? If I know, I will do what you say.

Odysseus
You shall be called a wise man and a good.

Neoptolemus
Well, then I will do it, casting aside all shame.

Odysseus
You clearly recollect all I have told you?

Neoptolemus
Yes, now that I have understood it.

Odysseus
Stay
and wait his coming here; I will go
that he may not spy my presence.
I will take with me to the ship this guard.
If you are too slow, I will send him back again,
disguise him as a sailor; Philoctetes
will never know him.
Whatever clever story he give you, then

fall in with it and use it as you need.
Now I will go to the ship and leave you in charge.
May Hermes, God of Craft, the Guide, for us
be guide indeed, and Victory and Athene,
the City Goddess, who preserves me ever.

(*Exit Odysseus.*)

Chorus

Sir, we are strangers, and this land is strange;
what shall we say and what conceal from this suspicious man?
Tell us.
For cunning that passes another's cunning
and a pre-eminent judgment lie with the prince,
in whose sovereign keeping is Zeus's holy scepter.
To you, young lord, all this has come,
all the power of your forefathers. Tell us now
what we must do to serve you.

Neoptolemus

Now—if you wish to see where he sleeps
on his crag at the edge—look, be not afraid.
But when the terrible wanderer returns,
be gone from the hut, but come to my beckoning.
Take your cues from me. Help when you can.

Chorus

Sir, this we have always done,
have kept a watchful eye over your safety.
But now
tell us what places he inhabits
and where he rests. It would not be amiss
for us to know this,
lest he attack us unawares.
Where does he live? Where does he rest?
What footpath does he follow? Is he in the house or not?

Neoptolemus

This, that you see, is his two-fronted house,
and he sleeps inside on the rock.

Chorus

Where is he gone, unhappy creature?

Neoptolemus

I am sure
he has gone to find food somewhere near here;
stumbling, lame, dragging along the path,
he is trying to shoot birds to prolong his miserable life.
This indeed, they say, is how he lives.
And no one comes near to cure him.

Chorus

Yes, for my part I pity him:
how unhappy, how utterly alone, always
he suffers the savagery of his illness
with no one to care for him,
with no friendly face near him,
but bewildered and distraught at each need as it comes.
God pity him, how has he kept a grip on life?

Woe to the contrivances of death-bound men,
woe to the unhappy generations of death-bound men
whose lives have known extremes!

Perhaps this man is as well born as any,
second to no son of an ancient house.
Yet now his life lacks everything,
and he makes his bed without neighbors
or with spotted shaggy beasts for neighbors.
His thoughts are set continually on pain and hunger.
He cries out in his wretchedness;
there is only a blabbering echo,
that comes from the distance speeding
from his bitter crying.

Neoptolemus

I am not surprised at any of this:
this is a God's doing, if I have any understanding.

These afflictions that have come upon him
are the work of Chryse, bitter of heart.
As for his present loneliness and suffering,
this, too, no doubt is part of the God's plan
that he may not bend against Troy
the divine invincible bow
until the time shall be fulfilled, at which it is decreed,
that Troy, as they say, shall fall to that bow.

Chorus

Hush.

Neoptolemus

What is it?

Chorus

Hush! I hear a footfall,
footfall of a man that walks painfully.
Is it here? Is it here?
I hear a voice, now I can hear it clearly,
voice of a man, crawling along the path,
hard put to it to move. It's far away,
but I can hear it; I can hear the sound well
the voice of a man wounded; it is quite clear now.

No more now, my son.

Neoptolemus

No more of what?

Chorus

Your plots and plans. He is here, almost with us.
His is no cheerful marching to the pipe
like a shepherd with his flock.
No, a bitter cry.
He must have stumbled far down on the path,
and his moaning carried all the way here.
Or perhaps he stopped to look at the empty harbor,
for it was a bitter cry.

Philoctetes

Men, who are you that have put in, rowing
to a shore without houses or anchorage?
What countrymen may I call you without offense?
What is your people? Greeks, indeed, you seem
in fashion of your clothing, dear to me.
May I hear your voice? Do not be afraid
or shrink from such as I am, grown a savage.
I have been alone and very wretched,
without friend or comrade, suffering a great deal.
Take pity on me; speak to me; speak,
speak if you come as friends.
No—answer me.
If this is all
that we can have from one another, speech,
this, at least, we should have.

Neoptolemus

Sir, for your questions, since you wish to know,
know we are Greeks.

Philoctetes

Friendliest of tongues!
That I should hear it spoken once again
by such a man in such a place! My boy,
who are you? Who has sent you here? What brought you?
What impulse? What friendliest of winds?
Tell me all this, that I know who you are.

Neoptolemus

I am of Scyrus that the sea surrounds;
I am sailing home. My name is Neoptolemus,
Achilles' son. Now you know everything.

Philoctetes

Son of a father—that I loved so dearly—
and of a country that I loved, you that were reared
by that old man Lycomedes, what kind of venture
can have brought you to port here? Where did you sail from?

Neoptolemus

At present bound from Troy.

Philoctetes

From Troy? From Troy!
You did not sail with us to Troy at first.

Neoptolemus

You, then, are one that also had a share
in all that trouble?

Philoctetes

Is it possible
you do not know me, boy, me whom you see here?

Neoptolemus

I never saw you before. How could I know you?

Philoctetes

You never heard my name then? Never a rumor
of all the wrongs I suffered, even to death?

Neoptolemus

I never knew a word of what you ask me.

Philoctetes

Surely I must be vile! God must have hated me
that never a word of me, of how I live here,
should have come home through all the land of Greece.
Yet they that outraged God casting me away
can hold their tongues and laugh! While my disease
always increases and grows worse. My boy,
you are Achilles' son. I that stand here
am one you may have heard of, as the master
of Heracles' arms. I am Philoctetes
the son of Poias. Those two generals
and Prince Odysseus of the Cephallenians
cast me ashore here to their shame, as lonely
as you can see me now, wasting with my sickness
as cruel as it is, caused by the murderous bite
of a viper mortally dangerous.

I was already bitten when we put in here
on my way from sea-encircled Chryse.
I tell you, boy, those men cast me away here
and ran and left me helpless. They were happy
when they saw that I had fallen asleep on the shore
in a rocky cave, after a rough passage.
They went away and left me with such rags—
and few enough of them—as one might give
an unfortunate beggar and a handful of food.
May God give them the like!
Think, boy, of that awakening when I awoke
and found them gone; think of the useless tears
and curses on myself when I saw the ships—
my ships, which I had once commanded—gone,
all gone, and not a man left on the island,
not one to help me or to lend a hand
when I was seized with my sickness, not a man!
In all I saw before me nothing but pain;
but of that a great abundance, boy.

Time came and went for me. In my tiny shelter
I must alone do everything for myself.
This bow of mine I used to shoot the birds
that filled my belly. I must drag my foot,
my cursed foot, to where the bolt
sped by the bow's thong had struck down a bird.
If I must drink, and it was winter time—
the water was frozen—I must break up firewood.
Again I crawled and miserably contrived
to do the work. Whenever I had no fire,
rubbing stone on stone I would at last produce
the spark that kept me still in life.
A roof for shelter, if only I have fire,
gives me everything but release from pain.

Boy, let me tell you of this island.
No sailor by his choice comes near it.

There is no anchorage, nor anywhere
that one can land, sell goods, be entertained.
Sensible men make no voyages here.
Yet now and then someone puts in. A stretch
of time as long as this allows much to happen.
When they have come here, boy, they pity me—
at least they say they do—and in their pity
they have given me scraps of food and cast-off clothes;
that other thing, when I dare mention it,
none of them will—bringing me home again.

It is nine years now that I have spent dying,
with hunger and pain feeding my insatiable
disease. That, boy, is what they have done to me,
the two Atridae, and that mighty Prince
Odysseus. May the Gods that live in heaven
grant that they pay, agony for my agony.

Chorus

In this, I too resemble your other visitors.
I pity you, son of Poias.

Neoptolemus

I am a witness,
I also, of the truth of what you say.
I know it is true. I have dealt with those villains,
the two Atridae and the prince Odysseus.

Philoctetes

Are you, as well as I, a sufferer
and angry? Have you grounds against the Atridae?

Neoptolemus

Give me the chance to gratify my anger
with my hand some day!
Then will Mycenae know and Sparta know
that Scyrus, too, breeds soldiers.

Philoctetes

Well said, boy!
You come to me with a great hate against them.
Because of what?

Neoptolemus

I will tell you, Philoctetes—
for all that it hurts to tell it—
of how I came to Troy and what dishonor
they put upon me.
When fatefully Achilles came to die. . . .

Philoctetes

O stop! tell me no more. Let me understand
this first. Is he dead, Achilles, dead?

Neoptolemus

Yes, he is dead; no man his conqueror
but bested by a god, Phoebus the archer.

Philoctetes

Noble was he that killed and he that died.
Boy, I am at a loss which to do first,
ask for your story or to mourn for him.

Neoptolemus

God help you, I would think that your own sufferings
were quite enough without mourning for those of others.

Philoctetes

Yes, that is true. Again, tell me your story
of how they have insulted you.

Neoptolemus

They came
for me, did great Odysseus and the man
that was my father's tutor, with a ship
wonderfully decked with ribbons. They had a story—
be it truth or lie—that it was God's decree
since he, my father, was dead, I and I only
should take Troy town.

This was their story. Sir, you can imagine
it did not take much time, when they had told it,
for me to embark with them.
Chiefly, you know, I was prompted by love of him,
the dead man. I had hope of seeing him
while still unburied. Alive I never had.
We had a favoring wind; on the second day
we touched Sigeion. As I disembarked,
all of the soldiers swarmed around me, blessed me,
swore that they saw Achilles alive again,
now gone from them forever. But he still lay
unburied. I, his mourning son, wept for him;
then, in a while, came to the two Atridae,
my friends, as it seemed right to do, and asked them
for my father's arms and all that he had else.
They needed brazen faces for their answer:
"Son of Achilles, all that your father had,
all else, is yours to take, but not his arms.
Another man now owns them, Laertes' son."
I burst into tears, jumped up, enraged,
cried out in my pain, "You scoundrels, did you dare
to give those arms that were mine to someone else
before I knew of it?" Then Odysseus
spoke—he was standing near me—"Yes, and rightly,"
he said, "they gave them, boy. For it was I
who rescued them and him, their former owner."
My anger got the better of me; I cursed him outright
with every insult that I knew, sparing none,
if he should take my arms away from me.
He is no way given to quarreling, but at this
he was stung by what I said. He answered:
"You were not where we were. You were at home,
out of the reach of duty. Since, besides,
you have so bold a tongue in your head, never
will you possess them to bring home to Scyrus."

There it was, abuse on both sides. But I lost
what should be mine and so sailed home. Odysseus,
that filthy son of filthy parents, robbed me.
Yet I do not blame him even so much as the princes.
All of a city is in the hand of the prince,
all of an army; unruly men become so
by the instruction of their betters.
This is the whole tale. May he that hates the Atridae
be as dear in the Gods' sight as he is in mine.

Chorus

Earth, Mountain Mother, in whom we find sustenance,
Mother of Zeus himself,
Dweller in great golden Pactolus,
Mother that I dread:
on that other day, too, I called on thee, Thou Blessed One,
Thou that rides on the Bull-killing Lions,
when all the insolence of the Atridae assaulted our Prince,
when they gave his arms, that wonder of the world,
to the son of Laertes.

Philoctetes

You have sailed here, as it seems, with a clear tally;
your half of sorrow matches that of mine.
What you tell me rings in harmony. I recognize
the doings of the Atridae and Odysseus.
I know Odysseus would employ his tongue
on every ill tale, every rascality,
that could be brought to issue in injustice.
This is not at all my wonder, but that Ajax
the Elder should stand by, see and allow it.

Neoptolemus

He is no longer living, sir; never, indeed,
if he were, would they have robbed me of the arms.

Philoctetes

What! Is he, too, dead and gone?

Neoptolemus

Yes, dead and gone. As such now think of him.

Philoctetes

But not the son of Tydeus nor Odysseus
whom Sisyphus once sold to Laertes,
they will not die; for they should not be living.

Neoptolemus

Of course, they are not dead; you may be sure
that they are in their glory among the Greeks.

Philoctetes

What of an old and honest man, my friend,
Nestor of Pylos? Is he alive? He used
to check their mischief by his wise advice.

Neoptolemus

Things have gone badly for him. He has lost
his son Antilochus, who once stood by him.

Philoctetes

Ah!
You have told me the two deaths that most could hurt me.
Alas, what should I look for
when Ajax and Antilochus are dead,
and still Odysseus lives, that in their stead
ought to be counted among the dead?

Neoptolemus

A cunning wrestler; still, Philoctetes,
even the cunning are sometimes tripped up.

Philoctetes

Tell me, by the Gods, where was Patroclus,
who was your father's dearest friend?

Neoptolemus

Dead, too.

In one short sentence I can tell you this.
War never takes a bad man but by chance,
the good man always.

Philoctetes

You have said the truth.
So I will ask you of one quite unworthy
but dexterous and clever with his tongue.

Neoptolemus

Whom can you mean except Odysseus?

Philoctetes

It is not he: there was a man, Thersites,
who never was content to speak once only,
though no one was for letting him speak at all.
Do you know if he is still alive?

Neoptolemus

I did not know him,
but I have heard that he is still alive.

Philoctetes

He would be; nothing evil has yet perished.
The Gods somehow give them most excellent care.
They find their pleasure in turning back from Death
the rogues and tricksters, but the just and good
they are always sending out of the world.
How can I reckon the score, how can I praise,
when praising Heaven I find the Gods are bad?

Neoptolemus

For my own part, Philoctetes of Oeta,
from now on I shall take precautions.
I shall look at Troy and the Atridae both
from very far off. I shall never abide
the company of those where the worse man
has more power than the better, where the good
are always on the wane and cowards rule.
For the future, rocky Scyrus will content me
to take my pleasure at home.
Now I will be going to my ship. Philoctetes,
on you God's blessing and goodbye. May the Gods

recover you of your sickness, as you would have it!
Let us go, men, that when God grants us sailing
we may be ready to sail.

Philoctetes

Boy, are you going,
going now?

Neoptolemus

Yes, the weather favors.
We must look to sail almost at once.

Philoctetes

My dear—I beg you in your father's name,
and in your mother's, in the name of all
that you have loved at home, do not leave me here
alone, living in sufferings you have seen
and others I have told you of.
I am not your main concern; give me a passing thought.
I know that there is horrible discomfort
in having me on board. Put up with it.
To such as you and your nobility,
meanness is shameful, decency honorable.
If you leave me here, it is an ugly story.
If you take me, men will say their best of you,
if I shall live to see Oetean land.
Come! One day, hardly one whole day's space
that I shall trouble you. Endure this much.
Take me and put me where you will,
in the hold, in the prow or poop, anywhere
where I shall least offend those that I sail with.
By Zeus himself, God of the Suppliants,
I beg you, boy, say "Yes," say you will do it.
Here I am on my knees to you, poor cripple,
for all my lameness. Do not cast me away
so utterly alone, where no one even walks by.
Either take me and set me safe in your own home,
or take me to Chalcedon in Euboea.

From there it will be no great journey for me
to Oeta or to ridgy Trachis or
to quick-flowing Spercheius,
and so you show me to my loving father.
For many a day I have feared that he is dead.
With those who came to my island I sent messages,
and many of them, begging him to come
and bring me home himself. Either he's dead,
or, as I rather think, my messengers
made little of what I asked them and hurried home.
Now in you I have found both escort and messenger;
bring me safe home. Take pity on me.
Look how men live, always precariously
balanced between good and bad fortune.
If you are out of trouble, watch for danger.
And when you live well, then consider the most
your life, lest ruin take it unawares.

Chorus

Have pity on him, prince.
He has has told us of a most desperate course run.
God forbid such things should overtake friends of mine.
And, prince, if you hate the abdominable Atridae
I would set their ill treatment of him
to his gain and would carry him
in your quick, well-fitted ship
to his home and so avoid offense before the face of God.

Neoptolemus

Take care that your assent is not too ready,
and that, when you have enough of his diseased company,
you are no longer constant to what you have said.

Chorus

No. You will never be able in this
to reproach me with justice.

Neoptolemus

I should be ashamed
to be less ready than you to render a stranger service.
Well, if you will then, let us sail. Let him
get ready quickly. My ship will carry him.

May God give us a safe clearance from this land
and a safe journey where we choose to go.

Philoctetes

God bless this day!
Man, dear to my very heart,
and you, dear friends, how shall I prove to you
how you have bound me to your friendship!
Let us go, boy. But let us first kiss the earth,
reverently, in my homeless home of a cave.
I would have you know what I have lived from,
how tough the spirit that did not break. I think
the sight itself would have been enough for anyone
except myself. Necessity has taught me,
little by little, to suffer and be patient.

Chorus

Wait! Let us see. Two men are coming.
One of them is of our crew, the other a foreigner.
Let us hear from them and then go in.

(*Enter the Sailor disguised as a Trader.*)

Trader

Son of Achilles, I told my fellow traveler here—
he with two others were guarding your ship—
to tell me where you were. I happened on you.
I had no intentions this way. Just by accident
I came to anchor at this island.
I am sailing in command of a ship outward bound
from Ilium, with no great company, for Peparethus—
a good country, that, for wine. When I heard
that all those sailors were the crew of your ship,

I thought I should not hold my tongue and sail on
until I spoke with you—and got my reward,
a fair one, doubtless. Apparently you do not know
much of your own affairs, nor what new plans
the Greeks have for you. Indeed, not only plans,
actions in train already and not slowly.

Neoptolemus

Thank you for your consideration, sir.
I will remain obliged to your kindness
unless I prove unworthy. Please tell me
what you have spoken of. I would like to know
what are these new plans of the Greeks.

Trader

Old Phoenix and the two sons of Theseus are gone,
pursuing you with a squadron.

Neoptolemus

Do they intend
to bring me back with violence or persuade me?

Trader

I do not know. I tell you what I heard.

Neoptolemus

Are Phoenix and his friends in such a hurry
to do the bidding of the two Atridae?

Trader

It is being done.
There is no delay about it. That you should know.

Neoptolemus

How is it that Odysseus was not ready
to sail as his own messenger on such
an errand? It cannot be he was afraid?

Trader

When I weighed anchor, he and Tydeus' son
were in pursuit of still another man.

Neoptolemus

Who was this other man that Odysseus himself should seek him?

Trader

There was a man—perhaps you will tell me first
who this is; and say softly what you say.

Neoptolemus

This, sir, is the famous Philoctetes.

Trader

Do not
ask me any further questions. Get yourself out,
as quickly as you can, out of this island.

Philoctetes

What does he say, boy? Why in dark whispers
does he bargain with you about me, this sailor?

Neoptolemus

I do not know yet what he says, but he must say it,
openly, whatever it is, to you and me and these.

Trader

Son of Achilles, do not slander me,
speaking of me to the army as a tattler.
There's many a thing I do for them and in return
get something from them, as a poor man may.

Neoptolemus

I am the enemy of the Atridae. This
is my greatest friend because he hates the Atridae.
You have come to me as a friend, and so you must
hide from me nothing that you heard.

Trader

Well, watch what you are doing, sir.

Neoptolemus

I have.

Trader

I put the whole responsibility
squarely upon yourself.

Neoptolemus

Do so; but speak.

Trader

Well, then. The two I have spoken of,
the son of Tydeus and the Prince Odysseus,
are in pursuit of Philoctetes.
They have sworn, so help them God, to bring him with them
either by persuasion or by brute force.
And this all the Greeks heard clearly announced
by Prince Odysseus; for he was much surer
of success than was the other.

Neoptolemus

What can have made
the Atridae care about him after so long—
one whom they, years and years since, cast away?
What yearning for him came over them? Was it the Gods
who punish evil doings that now have driven them
to retribution for injustice?

Trader

I will explain all that. Perhaps you haven't heard.
There was a prophet of very good family,
a son of Priam indeed, called Helenus.
He was captured one night in an expedition
undertaken singlehanded by Odysseus,
of whom all base and shameful things are spoken,
captured by stratagem. Odysseus brought
his prisoner before the Greeks, a splendid prize.
Helenus prophesied everything to them
and, in particular, touching the fortress of Troy,
that they could never take it till they persuaded
Philoctetes to come with them and leave his island.
As soon as Odysseus heard the prophet say this,
he promised at once to bring the man before them,
for all to see—he thought, as a willing prisoner,
but, if not that, against his will. If he failed,

"any of them might have his head," he declared. My boy,
that is the whole story; that is why I urge you
and him and any that you care for to make haste.

Philoctetes

Ah!
Did he indeed swear that he would persuade me
to sail with him, did he so, that utter devil?
As soon shall I be persuaded, when I am dead,
to rise from Death's house, come to the light again,
as his own father did.

Trader

I do not know about that. Well, I will be going now
to my ship. May God prosper you both!

(*Exit Trader.*)

Philoctetes

Is it not terrible, boy, that this Odysseus
should think that there are words soft enough to win me,
to let him put me in his boat, exhibit me
in front of all the Greeks?
No! I would rather listen to my worst enemy,
the snake that bit me, made me into this cripple.
But he can say anything, he can dare anything.
Now I know that he will come here.
Boy, let us go, that a great sea may sever
us from Odysseus' ship.
Let us go. For look, haste in due season shown
brings rest and peace when once the work is done.

Neoptolemus

When the wind at our prow falls, we can sail, no sooner.
Now it is dead against us.

Philoctetes

It is always fair sailing, when you escape evil.

Neoptolemus

Yes, but the wind is against them, too.

Philoctetes

For pirates
when they can thieve and plunder, no wind is contrary.

Neoptolemus

If you will, then, let us go. Take from your cave
what you need most and love most.

Philoctetes

There are some things I need, but no great choice.

Neoptolemus

What is there that you will not find on board?

Philoctetes

A herb I have, the chief means to soothe my wound,
to lull the pain to sleep.

Neoptolemus

Bring it out then.
What else is there that you would have?

Philoctetes

Any arrow
I may have dropped and missed. For none of them
must I leave for another to pick up.

Neoptolemus

Is this, in your hands, the famous bow?

Philoctetes

Yes, this,
this in my hands.

Neoptolemus

May I see it closer,
touch and adore it like a god?

Philoctetes

You may have it
and anything else of mine that is for your good.

Neoptolemus

I long for it, yet only with such longing

that if it is lawful, I may have it, else
let it be.

Philoctetes

Your words are holy, boy. It is lawful.
for you have given me, and you alone,
the sight of the sun shining above us here,
the sight of my Oeta, of my old father, my friends.
You have raised me up above my enemies,
when I was under their feet. You may be confident.
You may indeed touch my bow, give it again
to me that gave it you, proclaim that alone
of all the world you touched it, in return
for the good deed you did. It was for that,
for friendly help, I myself won it first.

Neoptolemus

I am glad to see you and take you as a friend.
For one who knows how to show and to accept kindness
will be a friend better than any possession.
Go in.

Philoctetes

I will bring you with me. The sickness in me
seeks to have you beside me.

Chorus

In story I have heard, but my eyes have not seen
him that once would have drawn near to Zeus's bed.
I have heard how he caught him, bound him on a running wheel,
Zeus, son of Kronos, invincible.
But I know of no other,
by hearsay, much less by sight, of all mankind
whose destiny was more his enemy when he met it
than Philoctetes', who wronged no one, nor killed
but lived, just among the just,
and fell in trouble past his deserts.
There is wonder, indeed, in my heart
how, how in his loneliness,

listening to the waves beating on the shore,
how he kept hold at all
on a life so full of tears.

He was lame, and no one came near him.
He suffered, and there were no neighbors for his sorrow
with whom his cries would find answer,
with whom he could lament the bloody plague
that ate him up.
No one who would gather
fallen leaves from the ground
to quiet the raging, bleeding sore,
running, in his maggot-rotten foot.
Here and there he crawled
writhing always—
suffering like a child
without the nurse he loves—
to what source of ease he could find
when the heart-devouring suffering gave over.

No grain sown in holy earth was his, nor other food
of all enjoyed by us, men who live by labor,
save when with the feathered arrows shot by the quick bow
he got him fodder for his belly.
Alas, poor soul,
that never in ten years' length
enjoyed a drink of wine
but looked always for the standing pools
and approached them.
But now he will end fortunate. He has fallen in
with the son of good men. He will be great, after it all.
Our prince in his seaworthy craft will carry him
after the fulness of many months, to his father's home
in the country of the Malian nymphs,
by the banks of the Spercheius,

where the hero of the bronze shield ascended
to all the Gods, ablaze in holy fire
above the ridges of Oeta.

Neoptolemus

Come if you will, then. Why have you nothing to say?
Why do you stand, in silence transfixed?

Philoctetes

Oh! Oh!

Neoptolemus

What is it?

Philoctetes

Nothing to be afraid of. Come on, boy.

Neoptolemus

Is it the pain of your inveterate sickness?

Philoctetes

No, no, indeed not. Just now I think I feel better.
O Gods!

Neoptolemus

Why do you call on the Gods with cries of distress?

Philoctetes

That they may come as healers, come with gentleness.
Oh! Oh!

Neoptolemus

What ails you? Tell me; do not keep silence.
You are clearly in some pain.

Philoctetes

I am lost, boy.
I will not be able to hide it from you longer.
Oh! Oh!
It goes through me, right through me!
Miserable, miserable!
I am lost, boy. I am being eaten up. Oh!

By God, if you have a sword, ready to hand, use it!
Strike the end of my foot. Strike it off, I tell you, now.
Do not spare my life. Quick, boy, quick.

(*A long silence.*)

Neoptolemus

What is this thing that comes upon you suddenly,
that makes you cry and moan so?

Philoctetes

Do you know, boy?

Neoptolemus

What is it?

Philoctetes

Do you know, boy?

Neoptolemus

What do you mean?
I do not know.

Philoctetes

Surely you know. Oh! Oh!

Neoptolemus

The terrible burden of your sickness.

Philoctetes

Terrible it is, beyond words' reach. But pity me.

Neoptolemus

What shall I do?

Philoctetes

Do not be afraid and leave me.
She comes from time to time, perhaps when she has had
her fill of wandering in other places.

Neoptolemus

You most unhappy man,
you that have endured all agonies, lived through them,
shall I take hold of you? Shall I touch you?

Philoctetes

Not that, above everything. But take this bow,
as you asked to do just now, until the pain,
the pain of my sickness, that is now upon me, grows less.
Keep the bow, guard it safely. Sleep comes upon me
when the attack is waning. The pain will not end till then.
But you must let me sleep quietly.
If they should come in the time when I sleep,
by the Gods I beg you do not give up my bow
willingly or unwillingly to anyone.
And let no one trick you out of it, lest you prove
a murderer—your own and mine that kneeled to you.

Neoptolemus

I shall take care; be easy about that. It shall not pass
except to your hands and to mine. Give it to me now,
and may good luck go with it!

Philoctetes

Here,
take it, boy. Bow in prayer to the Gods' envy
that the bow may not be to you a sorrow
nor as it was to me and its former master.

Neoptolemus

You Gods, grant us both this and grant us
a journey speedy with a prosperous wind
to where God sends us and our voyage holds.

Philoctetes

An empty prayer, I am afraid, boy:
the blood is trickling, dripping murderously
from its deep spring. I look for something new.
It is coming now, coming. Ah!
You have the bow. Do not go away from me.
Ah!
O man of Cephallenia, would it were you,
Would it were your breast that the pains transfix.
Ah!

Agamemnon and Menelaus, my two generals,
would it were your two bodies that had fed
this sickness for as long as mine has. Ah!

Death, death, how is it that I can call on you,
always, day in, day out, and you cannot come to me?
Boy, my good boy, take up this body of mine
and burn it on what they call the Lemnian fire.
I had the resolution once to do this for another,
the son of Zeus, and so obtained the arms
that you now hold. What do you say?
What do you say? Nothing? Where are you, boy?

Neoptolemus

I have been in pain for you; I have been
in sorrow for your pain.

Philoctetes

No, boy, keep up your heart. She is quick in coming
and quick to go. Only I entreat you, do not
leave me alone.

Neoptolemus

Do not be afraid. We shall stay.

Philoctetes

You will?

Neoptolemus

You may be sure of it.

Philoctetes

Your oath,
I do not think it fit to put you to your oath.

Neoptolemus

I *may* not go without you, Philoctetes.

Philoctetes

Give me your hand upon it.

Neoptolemus
Here I give it you,
to remain.

Philoctetes
Now—take me away from here—

Neoptolemus
What do you mean?

Philoctetes
Up, up.

Neoptolemus
What madness is upon you? Why do you look
on the sky above us?

Philoctetes
Let me go, let me go.

Neoptolemus
Where?

Philoctetes
Oh, let me go.

Neoptolemus
Not I.

Philoctetes
You will kill me if you touch me.

Neoptolemus
Now I shall let you go, now you are calmer.

Philoctetes
Earth, take my body, dying as I am.
The pain no longer lets me stand.

Neoptolemus
In a little while, I think,
sleep will come on this man. His head is nodding.
The sweat is soaking all his body over,
and a black flux of blood and matter has broken
out of his foot. Let us leave him quiet, friends,
until he falls asleep.

Chorus

Sleep that knows not pain nor suffering
kindly upon us, Lord,
kindly, kindly come.
Spread your enveloping radiance,
as now, over his eyes.
Come, come, Lord Healer.

Boy, look to your standing,
look to your going, look to your plans
for the future. Do you see? He sleeps.
What is it we are waiting to do?
Ripeness that holds decision over all things
wins many a victory suddenly.

Neoptolemus

Yes, it is true he hears nothing, but I see we have hunted in vain,
vainly have captured our quarry the bow, if we sail without him.
His is the crown of victory, him the God said we must bring.
Shame shall be ours if we boast and our lies still leave victory unwon.

Chorus

Boy, to all of this the God shall look.
Answer me gently;
low, low, whisper,
whisper, boy.
The sleep of a sick man has keen eyes.
It is a sleep unsleeping.

But to the limits of what you can,
look to this, look to this secretly,
how you may do it.
You know of whom I speak.
If your mind holds the same purpose touching this man,
the wise can see trouble and no way to cure it.
It is a fair wind, boy, a fair wind:
the man is eyeless and helpless,

outstretched under night's blanket—
asleep in the sun is good—
neither of foot nor of hand nor of anything is he master,
but is even as one that lies in Death's house.
Look to it, look if what you say
is seasonable. As far as my mind,
boy, can grasp it, best is the trouble taken
that causes the least fear.

Neoptolemus

Quiet, I tell you! Are you mad? He is stirring,
his eyes are stirring; he is raising his head.

Philoctetes

Blessed the light that comes after my sleep,
blessed the watching of friends.
I never would have hoped this,
that you would have the pity of heart to support
my afflictions, that you should stand by me and help.
The Atridae, those brave generals, were not so,
they could not so easily put up with me.
You have a noble nature, Neoptolemus,
and noble were your parents. You have made light
of all of this—the offense of my cries and the smell.
And now, since it would seem I can forget
my sickness for a while and rest, raise me yourself,
raise me up, boy, and set me on my feet,
that when my weariness releases me,
we can go to the ship and sail without delay.

Neoptolemus

I am glad to see you unexpectedly,
eyes open, free of pain, still with the breath of life.
With suffering like yours, all the signs pointed
to your being dead. Now, lift yourself up.
If you would rather, these men will lift you. They
will spare no trouble, since you and I are agreed.

Philoctetes

Thanks, boy. Lift me yourself, as you thought of it.
Do not trouble them, let them not be disquieted
before they need by the foul smell of me; living
on board with me will try their patience enough.

Neoptolemus

Very well, then; stand on your feet; take hold yourself.

Philoctetes

Do not be afraid; old habit will help me up.

Neoptolemus

Now is the moment. What shall I do from now on?

Philoctetes

What is it, boy? Where are your words straying?

Neoptolemus

I do not know what to say. I am at a loss.

Philoctetes

Why are you at a loss? Do not say so, boy.

Neoptolemus

It is indeed my case.

Philoctetes

Is it disgust at my sickness? Is it this
that makes you shrink from taking me?

Neoptolemus

All is disgust when one leaves his own nature
and does things that misfit it.

Philoctetes

It is not unlike your father, either in word
or in act, to help a good man.

Neoptolemus

I shall be shown to be dishonorable:
I am afraid of that.

Philoctetes

Not in your present actions. Your words make me hesitate.

Neoptolemus

Zeus, what must I do? Twice be proved base,
hiding what I should not, saying what is most foul?

Philoctetes

Unless I am wrong, here is a man who will
betray me, leave me—so it seems—and sail away.

Neoptolemus

Not I; I will not leave you. To your bitterness,
I shall send you on a journey—and I dread this.

Philoctetes

What are you saying, boy? I do not understand.

Neoptolemus

I will not hide anything. You must sail to Troy
to the Achaeans, join the army of the Atridae.

Philoctetes

What! What can you mean?

Neoptolemus

Do not cry yet
until you learn.

Philoctetes

Learn what? What would you do with me?

Neoptolemus

First save you from this torture, then with you
go and lay waste the land of Troy.

Philoctetes

You would?
This is, in truth, what you intend?

Neoptolemus

Necessity,
a great necessity compels it. Do not be angry.

Philoctetes

Then I am lost. I am betrayed. Why, stranger,
have you done this to me? Give me back my bow.

Neoptolemus

That I cannot. Justice and interest
make me obedient to those in authority.

Philoctetes

You fire, you every horror, most hateful engine
of ruthless mischief, what have you done to me,
what treachery! Have you no shame to see me
that kneeled to you, entreated you, hard of heart?

You robbed me of my livelihood, taking my bow.
Give it back, I beg you, give it back, I pray, my boy!
By your father's Gods, do not take my livelihood.
He does not say a word,
but turns away his eyes. He will not give it up.

Caverns and headlands, dens of wild creatures,
you jutting broken crags, to you I raise my cry—
there is no one else that I can speak to—
and you have always been there, have always heard me,
Let me tell you what he has done to me, this boy,
Achilles' son. He swore to bring me home;
he brings me to Troy. He gave me his right hand,
then took and keeps my sacred bow,
the bow of Heracles, the son of Zeus,
and means to show it to the Argives,
as though in me he had conquered a strong man,
as though he led me captive to his power.
He does not know he is killing one that is dead,
a kind of vaporous shadow, a mere wraith.
Had I had my strength, he had not conquered me,
for, even as I am, it was craft that did it.
I have been deceived and am lost.
What can I do?

Give it back. Be your true self again. Will you not?
No word. Then I am nothing.

Two doors cut in the rock, to you again,
again I come, enter again, unarmed,
no means to feed myself! Here in this passage
I shall shrivel to death alone. I shall kill no more,
neither winged bird nor wild thing of the hills
with this my bow. I shall myself in death
be a feast for those that fed me. Those that I hunted
shall be my hunters now.
Life for the life I took, I shall repay
at the hands of this man that seemed to know no harm.

My curse upon your life!—but not yet still
until I know if you will change again;
if you will not, may an evil death be yours!

Chorus

What shall we do? Shall we sail? Shall we do as he asks?
Prince, it is you must decide.

Neoptolemus

A kind of compassion,
a terrible compassion, has come upon me
for him. I have felt for him all the time.

Philoctetes

Pity me, boy, by the Gods; do not bring on yourself
men's blame for your crafty victory over me.

Neoptolemus

What shall I do? I would I had never left
Scyrus, so hateful is what I face now.

Philoctetes

You are not bad yourself; by bad men's teaching
you came to practice your foul lesson. Leave it to others
such as it suits, and sail away. Give me my arms.

Neoptolemus

What shall we do, men?

(*Odysseus appears.*)

Odysseus

Scoundrel, what are you doing? Give me those arms.

Philoctetes

Who is this? Is that Odysseus' voice?

Odysseus

It is.

Odysseus certainly; you can see him here.

Philoctetes

Then I have been sold indeed; I am lost. It was he
who took me prisoner, robbed me of my arms.

Odysseus

Yes, I, I and no other. I admit that.

Philoctetes

Boy, give me back my bow, give it back to me.

Odysseus

That he will never
be able to do now, even if he wishes it.
And you must come with the bow, or these will
bring you.

Philoctetes

Your wickedness and impudence are without limit.
Will these men bring me, then, against my will?

Odysseus

Yes, if you do not come with a good grace.

Philoctetes

O land of Lemnos and all mastering brightness,
Hephaestus-fashioned, must I indeed bear this,
that he, Odysseus, drags me from you with violence?

Odysseus

It is Zeus, I would have you know, Zeus this land's ruler,
who has determined. I am only his servant.

Philoctetes

Hateful creature,
what things you can invent! You plead the Gods
to screen your actions and make the Gods out liars.

Odysseus

They speak the truth. The road must be traveled.

Philoctetes

I say No.

Odysseus

I say Yes. You must listen.

Philoctetes

Are we slaves and not free? Is it as such
our fathers have begotten us?

Odysseus

No, but as equals
of the best, with whom it is destined you must take Troy,
dig her down stone by stone.

Philoctetes

Never, I would rather suffer anything than this.
There is still my steep and rugged precipice here.

Odysseus

What do you mean to do?

Philoctetes

Throw myself down,
shatter my head upon the rock below.

Odysseus

Hold him. Take this solution out of his power.

Philoctetes

Hands of mine, quarry of Odysseus' hunting,
now suffer in your lack of the loved bowstring!

You who have never had a healthy thought
nor noble, you Odysseus, how you have hunted me,
how you have stolen upon me with this boy

as your shield, because I did not know him, one
that is no mate for you but worthy of me,
who knows nothing but to do what he was bidden,
and now, you see, is suffering bitterly
for his own faults and what he brought on me.
Your shabby, slit-eyed soul taught him step by step
to be clever in mischief against his nature and will.
Now it is my turn, now to my sorrow you have me
bound hand and foot, intend to take me away,
away from this shore on which you cast me once
without friends or comrades or city, a dead man among the living.

My curse on you! I have often cursed you before,
but the Gods give me nothing that is sweet to me.
You have joy to be alive, and I have sorrow
because my very life is linked to this pain,
laughed at by you and your two generals,
the sons of Atreus whom you serve in this.
And yet, when you sailed with them, it was by constraint
and trickery, while I came of my own free will
with seven ships, to my undoing, I
whom they dishonored and cast away—
you say it was they that did it and they you.

But now why are you taking me? For what?
I am nothing now. To you all I have long been dead.
God-hated wretch, how is it that now I am not
lame and foul-smelling? How can you burn your sacrifice
to God if I sail with you? Pour your libations?
This was your excuse for casting me away.

May death in ugly form come on you! It will so come,
for you have wronged me, if the Gods care for justice.
And I know that they do care for it, for at present
you never would have sailed here for my sake
and my happiness, had not the goad of God,

a need of me, compelled you.
Land of my fathers, Gods that look on men's deeds,
take vengeance on these men, in your own good time,
upon them all, if you have pity on me!
Wretchedly as I live, if I saw them
dead, I could dream that I was free of my sickness.

Chorus

He is a hard man, Odysseus, this stranger,
and hard his words: no yielding to suffering in them.

Odysseus

If I had the time, I have much I could say to him.
As it is, there is only one thing. As the occasion
demands, such a one am I.
When there is a competition of men just and good,
you will find none more scrupulous than myself.
What I seek in everything is to win
except in your regard: I willingly yield to you now.

Let him go, men. Do not lay a finger on him.
Let him stay here. We have these arms of yours
and do not need you, Philoctetes.
Teucer is with us who has the skill and I,
who, I think, am no meaner master of them
and have as straight an aim. Why do we need you?
Farewell: pace Lemnos. Let us go. Perhaps
your prize will bring me the honor you should have had.

Philoctetes

What shall I do? Will you appear
before the Argives in the glory of my arms?

Odysseus

Say nothing further to me. I am going.

Philoctetes

Your voice has no word for me, son of Achilles?
Will you go away in silence?

Odysseus

Come, Neoptolemus.
Do not look at him. Your generosity
may spoil our future.

Philoctetes

You, too, men, will you go
and leave me alone? Do you, too, have no pity?

Chorus

This young man is our captain. What he says to you
we say as well.

Neoptolemus (to the Chorus)

Odysseus will tell me
that I am full of pity for him. Still
remain, if he will have it so, as long
as it takes the sailors to ready the tackle
and until we have made our prayer to the Gods.
Perhaps, in the meantime, he will have better thoughts
about us. Let us go, Odysseus.
You, when we call you, be quick to come.

(*Exeunt Odysseus and Neoptolemus.*)

Philoctetes

Hollow in the rock, hollow cave, sun-warmed, ice cold,
I was not destined, after all, ever to leave you.
Still with me, you shall be witness to my dying.
Passageway, crowded with my cries of pain,
what shall be, now again, my daily life with you?
What hope shall I find of food to keep my wretched life alive?
Above me, in the clouds, down the shrill winds
the birds; no strength in me to stop them.

Chorus

It was you who doomed yourself,
man of hard fortune. From no other,
from nothing stronger, came your mischance.
When you could have chosen wisdom,

with better opportunity before you,
you chose the worse.

Philoctetes

Sorrow, sorrow is mine. Suffering has broken me,
who must live henceforth alone from all the world,
must live here and die here;
no longer bringing home food nor winning
it with strong hands: Unmarked, the crafty words
of a treacherous heart stole on me. Would I might see him,
contriver of this trap,
for as long as I am, condemned to pain.

Chorus

It was the will of the Gods
that has subdued you, no craft
to which my hand was lent.
Turn your hate, your ill-omened curses, elsewhere.
This indeed lies near my heart,
that you should not reject my friendship.

Philoctetes

By the shore of the gray sea he sits and laughs at me.
He brandishes in his hand the weapon which kept me alive,
which no one else had handled. Bow that I loved,
forged from the hands that loved you, if you could feel,
you would see me with pity, successor to Heracles,
that used you and shall handle you no more.
You have found a new master, a man of craft, and shall be bent
by him.
You shall see crooked deceits and the face of my hateful foe,
and a thousand ill things such as he contrived against me.

Chorus

A man should give careful heed to say what is just;
and when he has said it, restrain his tongue from rancor and taunt.
Odysseus was one man, appointed by many,
by their command he has done this, a service to his friends.

Philoctetes

Birds my victims, tribes of bright-eyed wild creatures,
tenants of these hills, you need not flee from me or my house.
No more the strength of my hands, of my bow, is mine.
Come! It is a good time
to glut yourselves freely on my discolored flesh.
For shortly I shall die here. How shall I find means of life?
Who can live on air without any of all that life-giving earth supplies?

Chorus

In the name of the gods, if there is anything that you hold in respect,
draw near to a friend that approaches you in all sincerity.
Know what you are doing, know it well.
It lies with you to avoid your doom.
It is a destiny pitiable to feed
with your body. It cannot learn how
to endure the thousand burdens with which it is coupled.

Philoctetes

Again, again you have touched my old hurt,
for all that you are the best of those that came here.
Why did you afflict me? What have you done to me?

Chorus

What do you mean by this?

Philoctetes

Yes, you have hoped to bring me
to the hateful land of Troy.

Chorus

I judge that to be best.

Philoctetes

Then leave me now at once.

Chorus

Glad news, glad news.
I am right willing to obey you.
Let us go now to our places in the ship.

Philoctetes

No, by the God that listens to curses, do not go,
I beseech you.

Chorus

Be calm!

Philoctetes

Friends, stay!
I beg you to stay.

Chorus

Why do you call on us?

Philoctetes

It is the God, the God. I am destroyed.
My foot, what shall I do with this foot of mine
in the life I shall live hereafter?
Friends, come to me again.

Chorus

What to do that is different
from the tenor of your former bidding?

Philoctetes

It is no occasion for anger
when a man crazy with storms of sorrow
speaks against his better judgment.

Chorus

Unhappy man, come with us, as we say.

Philoctetes

Never, never! That is my fixed purpose.
Not though the Lord of the Lightning, bearing his fiery bolts,
come against me, burning me
with flame and glare.
Let Ilium go down and all that under its walls
had the heart to cast me away, crippled!
Friends, grant me one prayer only.

Chorus

What is it you would seek?

Philoctetes

A sword, if you have got one,
or an ax or some weapon—give it me!

Chorus

What would you do with it?

Philoctetes

Head and foot,
head and foot, all of me, I would cut with my own hand.
My mind is set on death, on death, I tell you.

Chorus

Why this?

Philoctetes

I would go seek my father.

Chorus

Where?

Philoctetes

In the house of death.
He is no longer in the light.
City of my fathers, would I could see you.
I who left your holy streams,
to go help the Greeks, my enemies,
and now am nothing any more.

Chorus

I should have been by now on my way to the ship,
did I not see Odysseus coming here
and with him Neoptolemus.

(*Enter Odysseus and Neoptolemus in front of the cave, talking. Philoctetes withdraws into the cave.*)

Odysseus (*to Neoptolemus*)

You have turned back, there is hurry in your step.
Will you not tell me why?

Neoptolemus

I go to undo the wrong that I have done.

Odysseus

A strange thing to say! What wrong was that?

Neoptolemus

I did wrong when I obeyed you and the Greeks.

Odysseus

What did we make you do that was unworthy?

Neoptolemus

I practiced craft and treachery with success.

Odysseus

On whom? Would you do some rash thing now?

Neoptolemus

Nothing rash. I am going to give something back.

Odysseus

What? I am afraid to hear what you will say.

Neoptolemus

Back to the man I took it from, this bow.

Odysseus

You cannot mean you are going to give it back.

Neoptolemus

Just that. To my shame, unjustly, I obtained it.

Odysseus

Can you mean this in earnest?

Neoptolemus

Yes, unless
it is not in earnest to tell you the truth.

Odysseus

What do you mean, Neoptolemus, what are you saying?

Neoptolemus

Must I tell you the same story twice or thrice?

Odysseus

I should prefer not to have heard it once.

Neoptolemus

You can rest easy. You have now heard everything.

Odysseus

Then there is someone who will prevent its execution.

Neoptolemus

Who will that be?

Odysseus

The whole assembly
of the Greeks and among them I myself.

Neoptolemus

You are a clever man, Odysseus, but
this is not a clever saying.

Odysseus

In your own case
neither the words nor the acts are clever.

Neoptolemus

Still
if they are just, they are better than clever.

Odysseus

How can it be just to give to him again
what you won by my plans?

Neoptolemus

It was a sin,
a shameful sin, which I shall try to retrieve.

Odysseus

Have you no fear of the Greeks if you do this?

Neoptolemus

I have no fear of anything you can do,
when I act with justice; nor shall I yield to force.

Odysseus

Then we shall fight
not with the Trojans but with you.

Neoptolemus

Let that be as it will.

Odysseus

Do you see my hand,
reaching for the sword?

Neoptolemus

You shall see me do as much
and that at once.

Odysseus

I will let you alone;
I shall go and tell this to the assembled Greeks,
and they will punish you.

Neoptolemus

That is very prudent.
If you are always as prudent as this,
perhaps you will keep out of trouble.

(*Exit Odysseus.*)

I call on you, Philoctetes, son of Poias,
come from your cave.

(*Philoctetes appears at the mouth of the cave.*)

Philoctetes

What cry is this at the door?
Why do you call me forth, friends? What would you have?
Ah! This is a bad thing. Can there be some fresh mischief
you come to do, to top what you have done?

Neoptolemus

Be easy. I would only have you listen.

Philoctetes

I am afraid of that.
I heard you before, and they were good words, too.
But they destroyed me when I listened.

Neoptolemus

Is there no place, then, for repentance?

Philoctetes

You were just such a one in words when you stole my bow,
inspiring confidence, but sly and treacherous.

Neoptolemus

I am not such now. But I would hear from you
whether you are entirely determined
to remain here, or will you go with us?

Philoctetes

Oh, stop! You need not say another word.
All that you say will be wasted.

Neoptolemus

You are determined?

Philoctetes

More than words can declare.

Neoptolemus

I wish that I could have persuaded you.
If I cannot speak to some purpose, I have done.

Philoctetes

You will say it all
to no purpose, for you will never win my heart
to friendship with you, who have stolen my life
by treachery, and then came and preached to me,
bad son of a noble father. Cursed be you all,
first the two sons of Atreus, then Odysseus,
and then yourself!

Neoptolemus

Do not curse me any more.
Take your bow. Here I give it to you.

Philoctetes

What can you mean? Is this another trick?

Neoptolemus

No. That I swear by the holy majesty
of Zeus on high!

Philoctetes

These are good words,
if only they are honest.

Neoptolemus

The fact is plain.
Stretch out your hand; take your own bow again.

(*Odysseus appears.*)

Odysseus

I forbid it, as the Gods are my witnesses,
in the name of the Atridae and the Greeks.

Philoctetes

Whose voice is that, boy? Is it Odysseus?

Odysseus

Himself and near at hand.
And I shall bring you to the plains of Troy
in your despite, whether Achilles' son
will have it so or not.

Philoctetes

You will rue your word
if this arrow flies straight.

Neoptolemus

No, Philoctetes, no!
Do not shoot.

Philoctetes

Let me go, let go my hand, dear boy.

Neoptolemus

I will not.

(*Exit Odysseus.*)

Philoctetes

Why did you prevent me killing my enemy,
with my bow, a man that hates me?

Neoptolemus

This is not to our glory, neither yours nor mine.

Philoctetes

Well, know this much, that the princes of the army,
the lying heralds of the Greeks, are cowards
when they meet the spear, however keen in words.

Neoptolemus

Let that be. You have your bow. There is no further cause
for anger or reproach against me.

Philoctetes

None.
You have shown your nature and true breeding,
son of Achilles and not Sisyphus.
Your father, when he still was with the living,
was the most famous of them, as now he is of the dead.

Neoptolemus

I am happy to hear you speak well of my father
and of myself. Now listen to my request.
The fortunes that the Gods give to us men
we must bear under necessity.
But men that cling wilfully to their sufferings
as you do, no one may forgive nor pity.
Your anger has made a savage of you. You will not
accept advice, although the friend advises
in pure goodheartedness. You loathe him, think
he is your enemy and hates you.
Yet I will speak. May Zeus, the God of Oaths,
be my witness! Mark it, Philoctetes, write it in your mind.
You are sick and the pain of the sickness is of God's sending
because you approached the Guardian of Chryse,
the serpent that with secret watch protects
her roofless shrine to keep it from violation.
You will never know relief while the selfsame sun
rises before you here, sets there again,
until you come of your own will to Troy,
and meet among us the Asclepiadae,

who will relieve your sickness; then with the bow
and by my side, you will become Troy's conqueror.

I will tell you how I know that this is so.
There was a man of Troy who was taken prisoner,
Helenus, a good prophet. He told us clearly
how it should be and said, besides, that all Troy
must fall this summer. He said, "If I prove wrong
you may kill me."
Now since you know this, yield and be gracious.
It is a glorious heightening of gain.
First, to come into hands that can heal you,
and then be judged pre-eminent among the Greeks,
winning the highest renown among them, taking
Troy that has cost infinity of tears.

Philoctetes

Hateful life, why should I still be alive and seeing?
Why not be gone to the dark?
What shall I do? How can I distrust
his words who in friendship has counseled me?
Shall I then yield? If I do so, how come
before the eyes of men so miserable?
Who will say word of greeting to me?
Eyes of mine, that have seen all, can you endure
to see me living with my murderers,
the sons of Atreus? With cursed Odysseus?
It is not the sting of wrongs past
but what I must look for in wrongs to come.
Men whose wit has been mother of villainy once
have learned from it to be evil in all things.
I must indeed wonder at yourself in this.
You should not yourself be going to Troy
but rather hold me back. They have done you wrong
and robbed you of your father's arms. Will you go and help them
fight and compel me to the like?
No, boy, no; take me home as you promised.

Remain in Scyrus yourself; let these bad men
die in their own bad fashion. We shall both thank you,
I and your father. You will not then, by helping
the wicked, seem to be like them.

Neoptolemus

What you say
is reasonable; yet I wish that you would trust
the Gods, my word, and, with me as friend, fare forth.

Philoctetes

What, to the plains of Troy, to the cursed sons
of Atreus with this suffering foot of mine?

Neoptolemus

To those that shall give you redress,
that shall save you and your rotting foot from its disease.

Philoctetes

Giver of dread advice, what have you said!

Neoptolemus

What I see fulfilled will be best for you and me.

Philoctetes

And saying it, do you not blush before God?

Neoptolemus

Why should one feel ashamed to do good to another?

Philoctetes

Is the good for the Atridae or for me?

Neoptolemus

I am your friend, and the word I speak is friendly.

Philoctetes

How, then, do you wish to betray me to my enemies?

Neoptolemus

Sir, learn not to be defiant in misfortune.

Philoctetes

You will ruin me, I know it by your words.

Neoptolemus

Not I. You do not understand, I think.

Philoctetes

Do I not know the Atridae cast me away?

Neoptolemus

They cast you away; will, now again, restore you.

Philoctetes

Never, if of my will I must see Troy.

Neoptolemus

What shall we do, since I cannot convince you
of anything I say? It is easiest for me
to leave my argument, and you to live,
as you are living, with no hope of cure.

Philoctetes

Let me suffer what I must suffer.
But what you promised to me and touched my hand,
to bring me home, fulfil it for me, boy.
Do not delay, do not speak again of Troy
I have had enough of sorrow and lamentation.

Neoptolemus

If you will then, let us go.

Philoctetes

Noble is the word you spoke.

Neoptolemus

Brace yourself, stand firm on your feet.

Philoctetes

To the limit of my strength.

Neoptolemus

How shall I avoid the blame of the Greeks?

Philoctetes

Give it no thought.

Neoptolemus

What if they come and harry my country?

Philoctetes

I shall be there.

Neoptolemus

What help will you be able to give me?

Philoctetes

With the bow of Heracles.

Neoptolemus

Will you?

Philoctetes

I shall drive them from it.

Neoptolemus

If you will do what you say,
come now; kiss this ground farewell, and come with me.

(*Heracles appears standing on the rocks above the cave of Philoctetes.*)

Heracles

Not yet, not until you have heard
my words, son of Poias.
I am the voice of Heracles in your ears;
I am the shape of Heracles before you.
It is to serve you I come and leave my home among the dead.
I come
to tell you of the plans of Zeus for you,
to turn you back from the road you go upon.
Hearken to my words.

Let me reveal to you my own story first,
let me show the tasks and sufferings that were mine,
and, at the last, the winning of deathless merit.
All this you can see in me now.
All this must be your suffering too,
the winning of a life to an end in glory,
out of this suffering. Go with this man to Troy.

First, you shall find there the cure of your cruel sickness,
and then be adjudged best warrior among the Greeks.
Paris, the cause of all this evil, you shall kill
with the bow that was mine. Troy you shall take.
You shall win the prize of valor from the army
and shall send the spoils to your home,
to your father Poias, and the land of your fathers, Oeta.
From the spoils of the campaign you must dedicate
some, on my pyre, in memory of my bow.

Son of Achilles, I have the same words for you.
You shall not have the strength to capture Troy
without this man, nor he without you,
but, like twin lions hunting together,
he shall guard you, you him. I shall send Asclepius
to Ilium to heal his sickness. Twice
must Ilium fall to my bow. But this remember,
when you shall come to sack that town, keep holy in the sight of God.
All else our father Zeus thinks of less moment.
Holiness does not die with the men that die.
Whether they die or live, it cannot perish.

Philoctetes

Voice that stirs my yearning when I hear,
form lost for so long,
I shall not disobey.

Neoptolemus

Nor I.

Heracles

Do not tarry then.
Season and the tide are hastening you on your way.

Philoctetes

Lemnos, I call upon you:
Farewell, cave that shared my watches,
nymphs of the meadow and the stream,

the deep male growl of the sea-lashed headland
where often, in my niche within the rock,
my head was wet with fine spray,
where many a time in answer to my crying
in the storm of my sorrow the Hermes mountain sent its echo!
Now springs and Lycian well, I am leaving you,
leaving you.
I had never hoped for this.
Farewell Lemnos, sea-encircled,
blame me not but send me on my way
with a fair voyage to where a great destiny
carries me, and the judgment of friends and the all-conquering
Spirit who has brought this to pass.

Chorus

Let us go all
when we have prayed to the nymphs of the sea
to bring us safe to our homes.

OEDIPUS AT COLONUS

Translated by David Grene

INTRODUCTION

This play is generally dated about 408 or 407 B.C. The legendary action would fall between the end of *Oedipus the King* and the beginning of *Antigone,* but in a sense it is a sequel to both, for Sophocles seems to have drawn on his own characterization of Oedipus in the former and of Antigone, Ismene, and, in part, Creon in the latter.

The myth follows one variant concerning Oedipus' end, according to which, after being outcast from all other countries and his own, he was at last received by King Theseus of Athens at Sophocles' own birthplace, Colonus, in the territory of Attica. Creon pursued him there, tried to drag him away, and kidnapped his faithful daughters; Theseus intervened and rescued the girls. There Polyneices, his estranged son, came to ask his blessing and received only curses. There Oedipus miraculously passed from this world, to be established in the holy ground as a guardian spirit of Athens.

TRANSLATOR'S NOTE

The above introduction by Richmond Lattimore is another of the very useful short notices he wrote for this volume of selected tragedies. I have shortened it a little more, and would like to add an explanation for the appearance of a new translation of this play by myself in this volume.

The original translation in the series was by Robert Fitzgerald. It was graceful and often very apposite. But it was in many respects far from literal. In verse renderings of the Greek plays, or for that matter in prose, one is ever and again sinning against a literalness which we all seek. But Fitzgerald's deviations from literalness are very marked indeed. Frequently they come through embellishment. At line 93 of the Greek text of the play the Greek says, "[He told me] that portents would come which would guarantee me this—earthquakes, some kind of thunder or the brightness [*Dios selas*] of Zeus." Fitzgerald renders "Earthquake, thunder, or God's *smiling lightning*." A little further on, Oedipus appeals to the Goddesses to give his terrible life some consummation, some term, and the Greek, rather touchingly, adds "unless I seem to you somehow of no account" [*ei mē dokō ti meinōs echein*]. Fitzgerald translates this "Unless indeed I seem *not worth your grace*." In both these cases, the "smiling lightning" and "not worth your grace," Fitzgerald has introduced a completely new idea, and one moreover which I think is very probably alien to Greek feeling.

It is of course unfair to stigmatize a whole translation on the strength of a few such small faults, if faults they are to be considered. Perhaps, as time goes on, one grows more crochety in one's judgment of imaginative work, especially in examining the details of it. Perhaps, more legitimately, some of the kinds of phrase, some features of the style of fifty years ago, often seem inappropriate to a theatrical piece intended for a modern audience. In any case, presumptuously or otherwise, I decided to try to translate this play again on my own. Whether I have improved it for present readers or not is up to them to decide.

A comparison of the numbered lines in the Greek text and those of my translation will show some discrepancies. In this play I found at times that it was impossible to match the two versions line by line, so I have renumbered the lines according to my English translation rather than the original Greek text. I thought that in a class today when the teacher wished to cite a line he or she would more usually want to do that for the students from the English at which the students were looking rather than from the Greek. I trust this will not lead to too much confusion. The differences tend to be only a matter of a few lines.

CHARACTERS

Oedipus

Antigone

A Stranger

Ismene

Theseus

Creon

Polyneices

A Messenger

Chorus

OEDIPUS AT COLONUS

(Enter Oedipus, now a very old man, accompanied by his daughter Antigone.)

Oedipus

I am blind and old, Antigone, my child.
What country have we come to? Whose is this city?
Who will today receive the wandering
Oedipus, with the scantiest of gifts?
It's little I ask for, and still less I get,
yet it is enough for me.
My sufferings have taught me to endure—
and how long these sufferings have lasted!—
and my high breeding teaches me the same.

Child, do you see anywhere I could sit,
either on the common ground or in the groves
belonging to the god? Set me there securely,
that we may find out where we are; we have come to be learners
as foreigners from citizens, to do as we are told.

Antigone

My poor suffering father, Oedipus!
there are towers here that protect the city; they look,
to my eyes, far off. This place is sacred—
as I would guess—it's thick with laurel,
with olives and with vines; the nightingales are singing,
thick-feathered, happily, inside the grove.
Here's a rough rock; bend and sit down on it.
This has been a long journey for an old man like you.

Oedipus

Set me now in place, watch over the blind man.

Antigone

I do not need to learn that now;
time has seen to that.

Oedipus

Can you tell me where we are?

Antigone

Athens—that much I know—but not this place.

Oedipus

Yes, Athens; every traveler has told us that.

Antigone

Shall I go and try to find which this place is?

Oedipus

Yes, child, if indeed there are people in it.

Antigone

People there are; I think I need do nothing.
I see a man now, near us.

Oedipus

Are you sure? Is he really coming this way?

Antigone

He is, indeed—here with us. Whatever you have
that is suitable to say, say it; the man is here.

Oedipus

Sir, I have heard her say—
she has eyes for both of us—that you have come
to inquire about us. Very opportunely
you come to clear up our uncertainty.

Stranger

Before you ask any more—up from this place
where you are sitting! This is no ground to tread on.

Oedipus

What is this place? What god is thought to possess it?

Stranger

It is inviolable, none may live in it. The Goddesses
most dreadful, the daughters of Earth and Darkness, possess it.

Oedipus

May I hear their sacred name to pray to them?

Stranger

The all-seeing Eumenides, the people here call them,
but they have other fair names elsewhere.

(A silence, broken by Oedipus' words.)

Oedipus

May they be gracious and receive their suppliant.
For I will never go from this land—from *this* place in it!

Stranger

What can you mean?

Oedipus

I have heard
the watchword of my destiny.

Stranger

No—I would certainly never have the boldness
to drive you out, without the city's sanction,
until I tell them what I am doing.

Oedipus

Sir, for God's sake, do not do me such dishonor—
poor wanderer that I am—to deny me
what I would beg you tell me.

Stranger

Then speak. I *shall* not do you such dishonor.

Oedipus

What *is* this place on which I have set foot?

Stranger

If you listen, I will tell you, whatever it is
I know myself. All of this place is sacred;

our holy lord Poseidon holds it. In it
there dwells Prometheus the Titan, fire-bearing god.
Within this land the spot you tread on
is the Bronze Road—so it is called—
it is the founding stone of Athens; the neighboring acres
boast that their ruler is the Knight Colonus
and all the people here bear his name in common.
That is how things are, sir; here is no mere honor in word;
the honor comes of living with the place, as theirs.

Oedipus

There are some, then, that live within this place?

Stranger

Yes, surely, those that are called by the god's name.

Oedipus

Have they a sovereign, or does the word rest with the people?

Stranger

They are ruled by the city's king.

Oedipus

And who is he
that is so mighty both in power and word?

Stranger

His name is Theseus, son of Aegeus, that was.

Oedipus

Can a messenger go from you to him?

Stranger

What for?
To tell him what, to urge his coming here?

Oedipus

That by small help he may reap great gains.

Stranger

Can a blind man give such help?

Oedipus

There shall be sight in all the words I say.

Stranger

Let me tell you, sir, how you will make no mistake;
You are noble—anyone can see that—in all but fortune.
Remain here where I first saw you, until I go
and tell my fellow citizens; not those in the city,
but citizens of *this* place. They are those to judge
whether you should stay here or again take the road.

Oedipus

Child, is the stranger gone?

Antigone

Yes, he is gone;
so, father, you may freely say everything,
for only I am by.

(Oedipus turns towards the grove and addresses those in it.)

Oedipus

O solemn, dreadful-faced Ones,
since first in this land with you I found my resting place
and bent the knee there, be not unmindful
of Phoebus and of me!
For Phoebus when he prophesied those horrors,
those many horrors for me, yet said that at the last
I should find rest here, in this final country,
when I should gain the haunt of the Dread Goddesses,
a place of hospitality for strangers.
There I should round my wretched life's last lap,
a gain for those that settled me, received me,
but a curse to those that drove me out.
As warranty of this there should come signs,
earthquakes and thunder, Zeus' lightning.
Now I know well that I can trust your omen
that guided me to this grove! Never, else, surely,
had I in my traveling met with *you* first of all,
I dry-mouthed, you that use no wine. Nor had I
sat on this sacred undressed rock. But, Goddesses,

as Phoebus' mouth has spoken, give my life ending
at last, some consummation of my course,
unless I seem to you inconsequential,
a slave to toils, the greatest in the world.
Come, you sweet daughters of ancient Darkness,
come, city, called after great Pallas,
Athens, most full of honor of any city,
pity this wretched shade of the man Oedipus;
the body that once was Oedipus is no more.

Antigone

Hush! Here are some old men coming
to spy out where we are resting.

Oedipus

I will be silent.
Do you conceal me in the grove, out of the way,
till I can find out what they will say; if we only hear,
we can be cautious in our actions.

Chorus of old men, nobles of Athens

Look! Who was he? And where?
Where has he disappeared? Where has he hurried,
man of most impious daring? Look for him, search for him,
inquire everywhere! Some wandering tramp
he must be, not from hereabouts; else he had never
set foot within this sacred grove
of those violent virgins whom we tremble to name,
whose dwelling place we pass
with no eyes to look, and without voice to speak,
with silent guard on lips, that no words
may a pious mouth sound forth.

But now the story goes that someone has come
who shows no reverence at all,
and search as I may I cannot discover
who he may be.

Oedipus

I am he; for I see
by the sound of a voice, as the proverb runs.

Chorus

Someone terrible to see,
terrible to hear.

Oedipus

Do not see me as a lawbreaker—
that I entreat you.

Chorus

Zeus the Defender, who can this old man be?

Oedipus

Surely no one to congratulate
on prime good fortune, guardians of this land.
I can be clear on that; else others' eyes
would not so guide my erring steps,
else had my greatness not found its anchor
on those that are but little.

Chorus

Woe for your blinded eyes! Were you so from birth?
Old and unfortunate
is how you look to us.
But at least if it lies with me,
you should not add another curse on yourself.
You advance too far, too far! Take heed
lest you stumble on that grassy stretch
where the mixing bowl
mixes its water with the stream that runs
sweetened with honey.
Unlucky stranger, watch heedfully. Away!
Step right away! He is too far away to hear!
Do you hear, you sorrowful wanderer?

If you want to speak and answer us,
leave that forbidden place and speak
where all may speak. Till then be silent.

Oedipus

Daughter, what should one think of this?

Antigone

Father, we must do as other citizens here,
yielding in what is dutiful, hearing with obedience.

Oedipus

Reach out your hand to me.

Antigone

Here do I reach it out.

Oedipus

Sirs, let me not meet with injustice
now I have trusted you and moved my ground.

Chorus

Old man, no one shall lead you
against your will, from where you rest at present.

Oedipus

Must I go further still?

Chorus

Still further.

Oedipus

Still further?

Chorus

Lead him, girl,
somewhat further. *You* are listening to me.

[*R. C. Jebb, the main English commentator on Sophocles, thinks that here there are three lines lost, in interchanges between Oedipus and Antigone.*]

Antigone

Follow me then, follow me
with your blind steps; follow where I lead you.

[*Jebb thinks that a line is lost here also.*]

Chorus

You are a stranger in a strange land,
poor man. Make your mind up
to reject what this city dislikes,
and reverence what she loves.

Oedipus

Lead me on, child,
to where, my feet once more on pious footing,
I may speak and hear.
We must not fight against necessity.

Chorus

Here, do not bend your steps
beyond this block of natural stone.

Oedipus

Is this as you want it?

Chorus

Far enough, I tell you.

Oedipus

May I sit?

Chorus

Yes, sideways, on the edge of the rock,
crouch low.

Antigone

Father, let me help you—this is my task—
step evenly with me.
Lean your old body on my arm that loves it.

(*Oedipus groans.*)

Oedipus
Oh, for the mischief that haunts my mind!

Chorus
Poor man, now that you rest,
tell me—who are you?
Who are you that is led so sorrowfully?
May we ask what is your country?

Oedipus
Sirs, I have no city; please do not—

Chorus
Do not do what, old man?

Oedipus
Do not ask who I am; do not push further
in your inquiry.

Chorus
Why so?

Oedipus
My breeding is full of terror.

Chorus
Tell me.

Oedipus
Daughter, what am I to say?

(He breaks into a sob.)

Chorus
Tell me what stock you are of, sir, and your father.

Oedipus (sobbing)
What will become of me, child?

Antigone
Tell them. You are as far as you can go.

Oedipus
I will tell them, then. Indeed, I cannot hide it.

Chorus
You are slow and hesitant. Be quick and tell us.

Oedipus
Do you know a son
of Laius?

Chorus
Oh, yes, yes!

Oedipus
He was of the family of the Labdacids.

Chorus
O Zeus!

Oedipus
The miserable Oedipus.

Chorus
And you are *he*?

Oedipus
Do not be so terrified
at what I say.

Chorus
(*cries out*)

Oedipus
A doomed man.

Chorus
(*cries out*)

Oedipus
Daughter,
what will become of me *now*?

Chorus
Out of this place, out of it!

Oedipus

And your promise? What will that be?

Chorus

Punishment is not the due lot of anyone
who but requites what is already done to him.
Trickery matching others' trickery gives
pain and not pleasure in return.
Up from this place!—and from this country where
you have found an anchorage!
Do not fix upon my city
some further debt to bear.

Antigone

Sirs, you have honor in your hearts,
but you cannot bear with my father, old and blind,
because you have heard the tale
of acts done in unconsciousness!
Yet, sirs, take pity on my wretched self;
I who beg you for my father only.
I beg you, with eyes not blinded, facing your eyes,
as though I came of your own blood,
that he, in his unhappiness, win your mercy.
What happens to us lies in your hands,
as though you were a god.
Come, grant me a favor—though I scarce look for it—
I entreat you by all that is dear to you—
by child or wife, by duty or by god.
No matter where you look, you will find no man
who can escape if a god leads him on.

Chorus

Why, know, you child of Oedipus, that you and he
both win our pity for your calamity.
But we dread judgment from the gods. We cannot
say more than what we have said to you already.

Oedipus

What is the good of a glorious reputation

if it is like an idly flowing stream?
They say that Athens is the holiest of cities,
say that she always rescues the injured stranger,
that she alone is able to defend him.
Where are these things for me? You moved me out
from the safety of this rock; then drive me out
forth from your country—fearing my name alone!
Surely not what I am nor what I have done.
Indeed, what I have done
is suffering rather than doing, if I were to tell you
the story of both my parents, which makes you dread me.
That I know well. How can my nature be evil,
when all I did was matching others' actions?
Even had I done what I did full consciously,
even so, I would not have been evil.
But the truth is, I knew nothing
when I came where I did. Yet *they* knew—
those by whom I suffered—knew what they did.
It was meant to be my death.
Therefore, sirs, I beseech you by the gods,
since you took me from my place of safety, save me now.
Do not, as honoring the gods, fail to give those gods
their dues of recognition. Think that they look
upon those that respect the gods and those
who do not so—among all men in the world.
Never yet has the wicked man got clear away,
escaping them. Take the side of those gods, do not dim the glory
of Athens by serving deeds of wickedness.
Rescue me, guard me; do not see the ugliness
of my face to its dishonor.
I am here as sacred and pious both,
and bringing benefit to your citizens.
When your lord comes here—whoever is your leader—
you shall hear all and understand it all.
In the time between these words and his arrival
do not turn villains.

Chorus

We needs must fear, old man, those haunted thoughts
coming from you; the words that clothe them are not light.
It is enough for me that this land's princes
shall know the matter through and through.

Oedipus

Sirs, where is the ruler of this land?

Chorus

He is in his father's city, in our country.
The man who sent me here has gone to fetch him.

Oedipus

Do you believe that he will care so much
to give a thought to a blind man—that he will come
himself to see me?

Chorus

He surely will when he has heard your name.

Oedipus

Who is there that will bring *that* word to him?

Chorus

It is a long road here; there are many travelers
and many tales of theirs; these he will hear
and come; do not trouble for that. Your name, old man,
has pierced the ears of many; were he asleep
or slow to move, yet when he hears
of *you*, he will come quickly to this place.

Oedipus

Well, may he come, with good luck for this city,
and for me, too! For what good man is there
who is no friend to himself?

Antigone

Zeus, what shall I say? What am I to think, father?

Oedipus

What is it, Antigone, my child?

Antigone

I see a girl
coming towards us riding an Etnean horse;
on her head is a Thessalian bonnet
which shields her from the sun. What do I say?
Is it really she? or not? does my mind cheat me?
It is—it isn't—I cannot tell—
It *is* she and no other. Her eyes are all aglow
as she comes to welcome me. That shows it is she—
she and no other, Ismene, my darling!

Oedipus

What is it you say, child?

Antigone

That I see your daughter,
my own sister. Soon you will know,
hearing her voice.

Ismene

Dear father and sister—how sweet are both those names!
How hard it was to find you, and now you are found,
how hard, again, to see you, for my tears!

Oedipus

You have really come, my child?

Ismene

Father—how hard to see you so!

Oedipus

You are really there, child!

Ismene

Yes, though it was hard to come here.

Oedipus

Touch me, my child.

Ismene

I touch you both alike.

Oedipus
Sisters. True sisters both!

Ismene
How wretched this life of ours.

Oedipus
You mean, her life and mine?

Ismene
Yes, and mine too.

Oedipus
Why have you come?

Ismene
Through care of you.

Oedipus
Because you longed to see me?

Ismene
Yes, and to tell you things
with my own tongue. My companion here
was the only trusty servant that I have.

Oedipus
Where are those brothers of your blood
to do us service now?

Ismene
They are where they are.
This is a terrible time for them.

Oedipus
Those two are like in everything
to the ways of Egypt,
both in their nature and in how they live.
For in that country the men sit within doors
working at the loom, while the wives go out
to get the daily bread.
So, children, those two brothers of yours, who should

bear the stress and strain, keep house within, like girls,
and you, in their stead, struggle to bear my troubles.
You, Antigone, since you ceased to be a child,
and had grown strong enough, wandered with me always,
to your unhappiness, guiding an old man's steps.
Many a time you strayed in the wild woods,
without a bite to eat and barefoot;
many a wet day, many a burning sunlight
you toiled through; you never thought
of home or comfort in comparison
with the need to earn your father the means to live.
And you, Ismene, in the old time came to me
unknown to the Cadmeans, with all their oracles
that spoke about this carcass of mine.
You were my trusty guard when I was hunted
out of Theban land.
But now again what tale have you to tell me,
your father? What mission started you from your home?
I am very sure you are not empty-handed,
but carry with you some terror affecting me.

Ismene

What I endured in looking for you, father—
in trying to find where you were living—
let me leave alone. I do not want to suffer
twice over, in the doing and telling both.
But I have come here to declare to you
the evils that befell your unhappy sons.

At first their passionate wish—as it was Creon's—
was to leave the throne to him, and not pollute
the city further. They looked sensibly
at the old destruction that lay on their breeding,
which indeed beset your unlucky house.
But now stirred by some god
and by some sinfulness of mind themselves,

a deadly spirit of competition
has entered these thrice unhappy beings
to grasp the government and the monarchy;
and the younger born, his hot blood up,
would rob his elder brother Polyneices
of the throne and has banished him the country.
The elder, as rumor multiplied declares,
went into exile in hollow Argos,
and there took to himself a new marriage tie
and for new friends new fellow spearmen,
his aim that Argos should possess in honor
the land of Thebes or else exalt to heaven
the Theban power by the defeat of Argos.
This is no empty sum of words, my father;
they are deeds and terrible. At what point the gods
will pity your tribulations I cannot guess.

Oedipus

Did you really hope the gods would take any heed
of me, enough some day to rescue me?

Ismene

I do, my father, from these present oracles.

Oedipus

And what are they? What has been prophesied,
my child?

Ismene

That you shall one day be desired
by Thebes, yes, living and dead you *shall* be,
for their own welfare's sake.

Oedipus

How can anyone's welfare depend
on such as I am?

Ismene

With you, they say, there rests
their victory.

Oedipus
When I *am* no longer
then am I a man?

Ismene
Yes, father, for today the gods exalt you;
then they destroyed you.

Oedipus
It is a poor thing to exalt the old
when he fell in his youth.

Ismene
Still, you must know that Creon
for these very causes is coming here,
and shortly, without loss of time.

Oedipus
What would he do,
my daughter? Explain that to me.

Ismene
They want to place you near the land of Thebes,
to own you, still not letting your foot tread
within the borders of their country.

Oedipus
What good can I do, lying outside their doors?

Ismene
The place you lie in—if it suffer wrong—
will be a heavy curse on them.

Oedipus
One needs no god to have the knowledge of that.

Ismene
Well, that is why they want to have you as an ally,
near to their land, but not as your own master.

Oedipus
Will they let the shadowing dust of Thebes lie on me?

Ismene

No, for the guilt of family bloodletting
debars it, father.

Oedipus

Then they will never own me.

Ismene

So shall there be a heavy weight of sorrow
upon the Thebans.

Oedipus

In what conjunction, child, shall this come to pass?

Ismene

When your anger strikes them, as they stand on your grave.

Oedipus

What you say now—from whom did you hear that?

Ismene

The sacred envoys when they came back from Delphi.

Oedipus

And that was, truly, what Phoebus said about me?

Ismene

So the men said that came to Thebes from Delphi.

Oedipus

Did either of my sons know this about me?

Ismene

Both of them equally; both knew it well.

Oedipus

And then those villains, when they heard of it,
longed for me less than for this throne of theirs?

Ismene

I hate to hear that said, but I must bear it.

Oedipus

Then may the gods never quench their fated quarrel
and may it lie in *my* hands to determine

the end of the fight, which now they seek so eagerly
with their raised spears. If that shall happen
neither he that presently holds throne and scepter
shall remain where he is; nor he the exile
shall return home. I am their father
and when I was dishonored and driven out
from my own land, they never hindered it,
nor helped defend me; as far as they could do it,
it was those two expelled me; by them I was proclaimed exile.
You might say that *then* I also willed it so,
and that the city granted me that gift.
This is not so; for on the day itself
when my spirit seethed, and death was dearest to me,
yes, death by stoning, no one would help me to it.
But when time had gone by,
and all the agony had mellowed,
when I felt my agony had outrun itself
in punishing my former sins—it was then and then
the city drove me out—after all that time!—
in my despite—and these, these sons of mine,
could have helped me, their father, but they would not.
No, for the lack of one short word from them
I was banished, a beggar, to wander forever.
But it was from *these,* girls as they are,
as far as their nature could, I had my sustenance,
and ground to tread on without fear,
and the support of kinfolk.
Those other two, above their father's claims
chose sovereignty, wielding the scepter,
and their land's lordship. No, they will never win me
to be their ally, nor shall there ever come
profit to them from their reign in Thebes:
that I know well, both from Ismene's oracles,
which I now hear, and when I recollect
those of old days which Phoebus has accomplished
now in this time.

So let them send Creon to fetch me in,
or anyone else of power within their city,
for if you, my foreign friends, are willing,
backed by those solemn goddesses
that are your champions, to grant me your protection,
you will win for your city
a mighty service and for enemies, trouble.

Chorus

Oedipus, you certainly deserve pity,
yourself and your daughters; and since you add to the count
that you will be the savior of our country,
may I suggest to you thoughts perhaps useful?

Oedipus

Dear friend: do but be my champion,
and be assured I will do all you tell me.

Chorus

Make an atonement to those deities
you came to first, when you trespassed on their ground.

Oedipus

In what fashion shall I do it? Tell me, sirs.

Chorus

First bring a sacred draught from the everlasting
springs there; and let the hands that bring it be pure.

Oedipus

And when I take this draught unsullied—what then?

Chorus

There are bowls there, work of a skillful maker;
crown the top of each, and the handles at either side.

Oedipus

With twigs or flocks of wool—or how shall I do it?

Chorus

With a flock of wool, new shorn, from a ewe lamb.

Oedipus
Very well; after that what must I do?

Chorus
Pour your offerings, with your face towards the first dawn.

Oedipus
Shall I pour them from the vessels that you speak of?

Chorus
Yes, in three streams; the last must empty the bowl.

Oedipus
What shall I fill the third with before I set it?
Tell me that, too.

Chorus
With water and with honey.
Do not bring wine near it.

Oedipus
And when the dark-shading earth has drunk of it?

Chorus
Then with both hands, taking nine sprigs of olive,
lay them on it; and say this prayer over them.

Oedipus
That I would hear—that is the greatest thing!

Chorus
"As we call these the Kindly Ones, with kindly
hearts may they welcome this suppliant for his saving."
So pray, or those who speak for you.
But say the words inaudibly; do not raise your voice.
Then go away—and do not look behind you.
If you do this, I will stand by your side and welcome.
Otherwise, sir, I will fear on your behalf.

Oedipus
My children, you have heard the strangers who live here?

Antigone
We have heard; do you but tell us what to do.

Oedipus

I cannot go myself; I fail in strength
and sight, my double weakness.
One of you must go and do this thing,
for I think that one soul—be it but a well-wisher's—
can pay the debt for tens of thousands.
Quickly now; but do not leave me alone.
My body cannot move, lonely of help,
nor without guidance.

Ismene

I will go to do it.
But I must know where I should find the place.

Chorus

On the other side of the grove, girl. If you need anything,
a man lives there who will tell you.

Ismene

I will go to my task; Antigone,
stay here and guard our father; for a parent's sake,
whatever trouble there is—if there is any—
does not count.

Chorus

It is a dreadful thing, sir,
to awaken again an old ill that lies quiet.
Yet still I long to know—

Oedipus

What? What do you mean?

Chorus

Of the pain that besets your life,
so remediless, so wretched—

Oedipus

Do not, I beg you—
I am your guest; you were kind to me.
Do not lay bare my sufferings;
they are beyond shame.

Chorus

It is a story that has spread far;
it doesn't die out. I would like to hear the right of it.

Oedipus

(moans)

Chorus

Endure the pain, I say.

Oedipus

Oh, oh.

Chorus

Do as I beg you. I gave you what *you* asked.

Oedipus

I bore the worst of sufferings—but for deeds—
be God my witness!—done without knowledge.
In all this there was nothing of conscious choice.

Chorus

How was it?

Oedipus

It was the city bound me,
in utter ignorance, in a deadly marriage,
in fated ruin, that came with my wife.

Chorus

Was it then, as I hear,
that you filled your bed
with your mother to your infamy?

Oedipus

Oh, it is death to hear it said,
strangers. These two girls of mine—

Chorus

You mean—

Oedipus

Yes, my children, they are the two
curses upon me.

Chorus

Zeus!

Oedipus

They sprang from the womb that bore me also.

Chorus

Then they are your children and—

Oedipus

Their father's sisters, too.

[*The passage that follows is difficult to understand. The Chorus has from the first, on hearing Oedipus' name, seemed to know the story. Apparently this may not be the case—at least the story in its entirety. There is another version of the myth, a fragment of Theban epic known to Pausanias, the very much later author of the geography of Greece, according to which the children of Oedipus here, Ismene and Antigone, are the children of his second wife, Euryganeia.* Odyssey XI 271 *is not explicit on this, but there are other aspects of its difference from our version—e.g., after Jocasta killed herself, Oedipus went on ruling Thebes. R. C. Jebb thinks it was the Attic dramatists who first introduced into the story the bearing of the incest on the daughters (Jebb, Commentary on* O.C. 534*). If this is right, the Chorus in the passage following this* does *make a genuinely new discovery from Oedipus. They may have been following till then the other and older version of the myth. The half lines of each speaker, each completing the statement, is far from anything we find dramatic. The whole is written in semi-lyrical meters and was probably delivered in a semi-ritualized manner, a kind of singsong interchange, almost like a dirge. It is of course extremely difficult for a translator to render tolerably.*]

Chorus

Oh, oh!

Oedipus

Ten thousand horrors sweep back upon me.

Chorus

You have suffered—

Oedipus

What I can never forget.

Chorus

But you *did*—

Oedipus

I *did* nothing.

Chorus

How can that be?

Oedipus

I received a gift
for serving the city—would to God I had never won it!—
for my heart is broken.

Chorus

Unhappy man! But you did a murder.

Oedipus

How a murder? What is it you would know?

Chorus

Your father's murder.

Oedipus

You strike me again, wound upon wound.

Chorus

But you killed him.

Oedipus

Yes, I killed him, but he had from me—

Chorus

What?

Oedipus

Something of justice.

Chorus

How can that be?

Oedipus

I will tell you.
Those that I killed would have killed me.
So in law I am innocent and came to all this
in ignorance.

Chorus

Here is our king, Theseus, son of Aegeus,
to do what the news of you summoned him to do.

Theseus

In time past, son of Laius, I have heard from many
of the bloody blinding of your eyes—and I recognized you.
Now as I heard more on my journey here
I am in greater certainty.
The clothes you wear and your unhappy face
show us clearly who you are. Because you have
my pity, unfortunate Oedipus, I would ask you
what is this supplication you urge on Athens
and on myself—you and the poor girl beside you?
Tell me. You must tell me something dreadful indeed
to make me turn away from you.
For my part I know what it means,
myself, to be brought up in exile,
as you are in exile. I too in a foreign country
wrestled with dangers to my life, more than anyone else.
So there is surely no stranger, such as you,
from whom I would turn my face, nor help to save.
For I am very certain I am but a man:
as such, I have of tomorrow no greater share
than you have.

Oedipus

Theseus, your nobleness in one short speech
has left me the necessity of saying little.
You have said about me all that is true—
who I am, from what father born, from what country come.

All that is left me to say is what I want,
and then the story is told.

Theseus

Tell me; let me know.

Oedipus

I come to give you this wretched carcass of mine,
a gift to you; to look at, no great matter,
but no beautiful body will give you such gains as it will.

Theseus

What is this gain you claim to bring with you?

Oedipus

In time you will know—but the time is not yet, I think.

Theseus

When will your benefit be shown?

Oedipus

When I die and you shall have been my burial man.

Theseus

You ask about the last moments of your life;
what lies between this and then
you either forget or have no heed of.

Oedipus

Yes:
when that is given, my whole harvest is in.

Theseus

The favor you ask me lies in small compass, then?

Oedipus

Watch that; it is no easy fight to win.

Theseus

Do you mean between your sons and me?

Oedipus

Yes.
They wish to carry me away to Thebes.

Theseus

Well, if you are willing—
exile is not a fine thing.

Oedipus

When I myself was willing they would not let me.

Theseus

You are being foolish; anger does not sit well
with folk in trouble.

Oedipus

Rebuke me when you understand, and not till then.

Theseus

Then tell me. True, without knowledge I should not speak.

Oedipus

I have suffered, Theseus, terribly, evils upon evils.

Theseus

You mean what befell your family from of old?

Oedipus

No. That is the talk of everyone in Greece.

Theseus

What then is your suffering beyond all men's endurance?

Oedipus

This is how it is. I was banished from my own country
by my own sons, return forever denied me,
because I killed my father.

Theseus

How then would they send for you
if it is but to settle you apart?

Oedipus

It is the mouth of God will force them to it.

Theseus

What is it, then, they fear foretold in oracles?

Oedipus

That they must be smitten by this land of yours.

Theseus

But how should there be bitterness between
them and myself?

Oedipus

O dearest son of Aegeus:
only the gods know neither age nor death;
everything else all-mastering time confounds.
The strength of earth, the strength of body, dies;
trust dies, distrust comes into blossoming.
The same breath does not blow from man to man,
constant in friendship, nor in city towards city.
It may be now, it may be later, sometime
the sweet turns bitter, and then again to friendship.
If now the day is bright betwixt you and Thebes,
uncounted time in course will breed uncounted
nights and days, shattering with the spear
those right hands presently clasped in harmony.
The cause will be so slight!
At that time my body hidden in earth and sleeping
will coldly drink their hot blood,
if Zeus be still Zeus and if Zeus' son
Phoebus speak clearly.
But it is not pleasant
to speak the words that should lie undisturbed.
Let me stop where I began; do you only keep
the pledge you gave me and you will never say
that you received as dweller in this land,
a worthless fellow, Oedipus—
unless the gods shall cheat me.

Chorus

My lord, this man has talked like this before,
as though he would do something for our country.

Theseus

Who would reject goodwill in such a man?
In the first place, forever a hearth between us
speaks of guest-friendship and a spear alliance.
And then he has come a suppliant of these Goddesses,
and promises to this land and myself
no inconsiderable recompense.
These matters claim my reverence and so
I will not reject his claim upon my gratitude.
I will make him our citizen. If it be his pleasure,
this stranger's, to remain here I will charge you
to guard him. (*Turning to Oedipus.*)
Or, if you please to come with me,
Oedipus, I submit to your judgment.
It shall be as you choose.

Oedipus

May God send blessings on such men as you!

Theseus

What would you, then? Will you come to my home?

Oedipus

I would—if it were lawful. But this place here—

Theseus

What would you do in "this place"? I will not oppose you.

Oedipus

It is *here* I will conquer those that cast me out.

Theseus

This would be a great gift of your staying here.

Oedipus

If you stand fast by what you said and do it.

Theseus

You need not fear for me. I will not fail you.

Oedipus

I will not put you on your oath like someone base.

Theseus

No oath will give you more than my bare word.

Oedipus

What will you do then—

Theseus

What is it you fear most?

Oedipus

Some will come here—

Theseus

My friends will take care of *that*.

Oedipus

See you do not fail me—

Theseus

Do not tell me my duty.

Oedipus

It is inevitable that I should fear.

Theseus

I do not fear.

Oedipus

You do not know the threats—

Theseus

I do know that no one
will take you out of here against my will.
There are many threats, and many threatening words
issue out of anger. When the mind is master of itself,
the threats have vanished.
Perhaps these people had strength enough to speak
dreadful things of your carrying off, but *I* know
the sea to sail between us will seem long,
poor prospects for a voyage. I would say to you
"Be of good cheer" even without my judgment,
since Phoebus sent you hither. Even though *I* were not here,
my *name* will guard you against ill-usage.

Chorus

Here are the fairest homesteads of the world,
here in this country, famed for its horses, stranger,
where you have come:
Here to Colonus, gleaming white,
where the nightingale in constant trilling song
cries from beneath the green leaves,
where she lives in the wine dark ivy
and the dark foliage of ten thousand berries,
safe from the sun, safe from the wind
of every storm, god's place, inviolable.
Where Dionysus the reveler paces
thronged by the nymphs his nurses.

Here there blooms, fed by heaven's dew,
daily and ever, the lovely-clustered narcissus,
the ancient crown of the Great Goddesses,
and also the golden gleaming crocus.
Nor fail the wandering springs
that feed the streams of Cephisus,
but daily and ever the river
with his pure waters gives increase
over the swelling bosom of the land.
This country the bands of the Muses
have not disdained
nor yet Aphrodite of the Golden Reins.
There is a thing too, of which no other like
I have heard in Asian land,
nor as ever grown in the great Dorian
island of Pelops,
a plant unconquered and self-renewing,
a terror that strikes the spear-armed enemy,
a plant that flourishes greatest here,
leaf of gray olive,
nourishing our children.

It shall not be rendered impotent
by the young nor by him that lives with old age,
destroying it with violence,
for the ever-living eye of Morian Zeus
looks upon it—and gray-eyed Athene also.

Yet another matter of praise have I
for this my mother city,
gift of a great god, our land's great boast,
that it is horse master, colt breaker, master of the sea.
Son of Cronus, Lord Poseidon,
you it is who have set her in that glory.
For you are the one who in these roads first
established the bit to control the horse,
and the oar, too, well fitted to the hand
leaps marvelously in the sea,
following the hundred-footed Nereids.

Antigone

Land with praises richly celebrated,
now be it yours to make those praises shine.

Oedipus

What is there new, child?

Antigone

Creon draws near.
Here he is—and with followers.

Oedipus (to the Chorus)

Old men,
my friends, now manifest, I beg you,
the last goal of my safety.

Chorus

Courage!
That safety shall be yours. If *I* am old,
the strength of Attica has not grown old.

Creon

Sirs, noble gentlemen of this land,
I see your eyes have suddenly taken fright
at my intrusion. I beg you, do not fear
nor speak ill words to me.
I have come with no determination
to offer any violence. I am old myself
and know I have come to a city powerful
as any is in Greece.
I was sent, old as I am, to urge this man
to come with me to Thebes.
No single person sent me. I have my orders
from the whole commonality. They sent *me*
because it was I who was most concerned
(because of our relationship) to sorrow,
most of all within our city, for *his* troubles.

Unhappy Oedipus, hear me and come home!
All the Cadmean people summon you, and rightly,
and most of all do I, in the proportion
that I must be the worst of scoundrels
if I felt no pain at these your sufferings.
I see you an unfortunate wretch, a foreigner,
a beggar always and your sightless journeyings
propped on this one girl only. I could not believe
that she could fall to such a depth of misery
as this unhappy child here, tending you
and your life in daily beggary, young as she is,
but with no part in marriage, a ready victim
to be seized and raped by anyone.
It *is* a miserable reproach, is it not?,
that I have cast on you—and on me and all our breed.
There is no hiding it. It's plain.
But, Oedipus, it is you—I beg you—by our fathers' gods, *you*,
listen to my words! it is *you* should hide it,
by willingness to come to your own city

and to the house that was your fathers'.
Greet this city kindly—of course she has deserved it!—
but your own country should be honored more,
in justice, for she bred you up at first.

Oedipus

You would dare anything; from every plea of justice
you can extract some means of trickery.
Why do you try so? Why do you want
to catch me once again, when the catching will hurt most?
In the old time I was so sick in my troubles
that it had been my pleasure to be exiled;
but then when I was willing, you were not
to give me any such favor. But when my anger
was sated of itself, when living in that house
had become sweet to me, you threw me out,
you banished me. In that day this kinship you speak of
was no way dear to you.
And now again, when you see this city friendly
to my staying, when you see all the people friendly,
you try to tear me out, the harshness of your message
so softly rendered!
Yet, what pleasure can you have in showing kindness
to those that will not welcome it? It is as if
one begged for something, but was given nothing,
nor was there wish to help; but when the spirit
was sated with what one had sought for, then only,
one got the gift, when the grace carried no grace.
Surely this is an empty pleasure you gain.
And that indeed is what you have given me,
where the words are good and the substance evil.
I will show these people what a villain you are.
You have come to bring me, yes, but *not* to bring me home
but to set me in a dwelling apart—but near you,
so there will be no trouble with Athens for your city.
You will not succeed, no, instead

my spirit shall dwell forever, a curse,
a curse upon your country.
For these sons of mine, this is my prayer—
so much of their father's earth as to make their graves.
Am I not wiser than you in Theban matters?
Far wiser, for I learn from clearer speakers,
Phoebus and Zeus himself, that is his father.
But you have come here, a mouth suborned,
but with a right sharp tongue. For all that, in your speaking
you will win more harm than safety.
However, I know I am not persuading you.
Get gone!
Let us live here; even as it is
we would live well enough
if we are content.

Creon

Who do you think has had the worst of it
in this discussion? I in respect to you
or you towards yourself?

Oedipus

What I find most pleasant is your failure
to persuade me or these men here.

Creon

You miserable creature, clearly you haven't
been able to grow wise, with all your years.

Oedipus

You have a clever tongue, but I never knew a just man
speak equally well on every plea.

Creon

Saying much is one thing, seasonableness another.

Oedipus

As though *your* words were few but very seasonable!

Creon

Not seasonable, of course, for one so clever
as you are.

Oedipus

Away with you! I will speak on these men's behalf;
do not watch and hem me in; this is where I live.

Creon

I call these men to witness, not you, for what you have answered
to those of us who are your family. If ever I catch you—

Oedipus

How will you catch me in despite of these allies?

Creon

I can hurt you enough without such action.

Oedipus

What lies behind these threats of yours?

Creon

You have
two daughters, one of whom I have seized
and sent away. The other I will take soon.

Oedipus

O God!

Creon

Soon you will have more reason to cry out.

Oedipus

You have my child?

Creon

And will have *this* one soon.

Oedipus

Sirs, what will you do? Will you betray your trust?
Will you not get rid of this unholy wretch?

Chorus

Here, you, sir, off with you! What you are doing
is utterly unjust. So is what you *have* done.

Creon (to his servants)

It is high time for you to lead her off.
If she won't go willingly, force her!

Antigone

What refuge have I? What help can I find
from god or man?

Chorus

What are you about, sir?

Creon

I will not take the man, but *she* is mine.

Oedipus

O, princes of this country!

Chorus

Sir, this is injustice!

Creon

No, it is just.

Chorus

How can it be just?

Creon

I take my own.

Oedipus

O city of Athens!

Chorus

What are you doing, sir? Release her at once.
If not—a trial of strength between us!

Creon

Give way!

Chorus

Not to you while this is your purpose.

Creon

You will fight with Thebes, if you do me an injury.

Oedipus

Did I not say
this is how it would be?

Chorus

Release that girl at once.

Creon

Do not give orders
that you cannot enforce.

Chorus

I tell you take your hands off her!

Creon

I tell you
take a walk!

Chorus

Come, countrymen of ours, come here, come here!
The city is made nothing of, our city,
by this violence. Come here, come here to us!

Antigone

Friends, I am dragged away.

Oedipus

Where are you, child?

Antigone

They are forcing me away!

Oedipus

Reach me your hands!

Antigone

I cannot I cannot.

Creon (to the servants)

Bring her away, you!

Oedipus
O God, O God!

Creon
Well, on these crutches you will not travel again.
But since you are determined to beat your country,
and your family at whose command I do
what I do—although I am their sovereign lord as well—
enjoy your victory. In time you will know,
I am certain, that what you do to yourself at present
is nothing good, nor what you did before,
when in the teeth of your friends you yielded to temper.
It is your temper which constantly ruins you.

Chorus
Stop right there, sir.

Creon
I warn you, do not touch me.

Chorus
Give back the girls. Else you will not go from here.

Creon
You will soon give my city a greater prize
for our security. I will take more than these.

Chorus
What will you do next?

Creon
I will take and carry *him* off.

Chorus
An outrageous threat!

Creon
It shall be executed.

Chorus
Unless this country's ruler thwarts you.

Oedipus
A shameless thing to say! Will you seize me indeed?

Creon

Hold your tongue!

Oedipus

May the gods of this place
not take away my tongue from uttering this curse!
You villain: after the violence to my onetime eyes,
you have wrenched from me the one poor eye I had left.
May the Sun-God that sees all give you and your seed
an old age like this of mine!

Creon

Do you see that, you people of this country?

Oedipus

They see both you and me; they understand
I am wronged in deeds, my defense, words only.

Creon

I'll not hold back my anger. I will bring him away by force,
although I am alone and slow with age.

Oedipus

(cries out)

Chorus

You have a bold spirit, sir, to think to come here,
and do as you do.

Creon

Yes, I believe I have.

Chorus

If you are right, I will no longer think
Athens a city.

Creon

With a just cause the weak subdue the strong.

Oedipus

Do you hear what he says?

Chorus

But he will not act it—
Zeus knows!

Creon

Zeus maybe knows—not you.

Chorus

The insolence of this!

Creon

Insolence you must put up with.

Chorus

You people, and the rulers of this state, come here to us!
Come quickly. These men will cross the border.

(Theseus enters.)

Theseus

What is this noise about? What has happened here?
You have stopped me in my sacrifice to the sea-god,
lord of Colonus here: I was at the altar.
What fear made you do that? Tell me. I want
to know it all, why I have been made to hasten
faster than I liked to this place here.

Oedipus

Dearest of men, I recognize your voice. I have suffered
dreadfully, right now, at this man's hands.

Theseus

What happened? Who has injured you? Speak!

Oedipus

Creon here, before your eyes, has taken my two
children, all that I had.

Theseus

What is this you say?

Oedipus

You have heard what he did to me.

Theseus (points to his servants)

Here, quickly, one of you go to the altars,
urge all the people to leave the sacrifice
and hurry, on horseback and on foot,
at a full gallop to that place hereabouts
where the two traveled roads combine,
so that the girls won't get across and I,
worsted by violence, become a mockery
to my guest-friend.
Away you go! Quickly! As I told you.
For you, Creon, if I went as far in anger
as you deserve, you would not go without
marks of my hands upon you.
However, such laws as he imported here
shall be made to fit him—these and no others.

(He speaks directly to Creon.)

You shall not leave this country until you bring here
these girls for me to see. What you have done
is a disgrace to me, and your own blood,
and to your country. You came within this city
that makes a practice of justice and determines
nothing without a law. You then throw aside
her lawful institutions by your invasion.
You take what you want, making them yours by force.
Apparently you thought this city quite unmanned
or some slave place, and me a nobody.
Yet it is not Thebes has taught you to be so bad.
They do not usually rear men as wrongdoers,
nor would the Thebans praise you if they heard
you had violated what are mine and the gods' possessions,
dragging out the helpless creatures that are their suppliants.
I certainly never would have put foot on your soil—

not if I had the justest cause in the world—
without permission of the governors, whoever.
I would not have harried and plundered; I would have known
how I ought—a foreigner among citizens—
to conduct myself. But you dishonor
a city that has not merited dishonor—
your own city; and your years, so many,
show you an old man still empty of wisdom.
So I tell you now what I have said before;
let someone bring those girls here—quickly, too—
unless you want to be a resident alien
of Athens, under constraint, not voluntarily.
That is what I have to say. It comes from my full meaning,
not simply from my tongue.

Chorus

You see what you have come to, sir. You appear
to be of those who are just, but what you do
is found to be evil.

Creon

Of course I did not think this city unmanned,
son of Aegeus, nor yet without wisdom as you claim,
when I did this thing I did. I thought
that no one would ever feel such eager love
for those that are my kinfolk that they would keep them
against my wishes! I knew you would not accept
a man who is his father's killer, unholy,
nor one whose marriage is found accursed,
a union of mother and son.
I knew the Areopagus, that grave council
which belongs to this country, would not permit
such outcasts as these to live within its realm.
It was because I was confident of this
that I laid my hands upon this quarry.
Even then I would not have done so had he not cursed me

myself with bitter curses, and my breed.
This is what he did to me, and I determined
to give as good again. Anger knows no old age,
except in death. No sting touches the dead.
That is the case; do as you will about it.
However just my cause, I am all alone;
that makes me weak; but yet as you shall act,
old as I am, I will try to act against you.

Oedipus

Spirit lost to shame, whom does the insult light on,
on you or me since both of us are old?
Your mouth is wide with taunts against me—murders,
and incest and calamity, which I bore,
poor wretch, involuntarily: the gods' pleasure!
Perhaps they were angry against my people of old.
You cannot find in me, taken by myself,
an offense to reproach me with of such a greatness
to occasion such dreadful sins as I committed
against me and mine.

Tell me this:
if some god-utterance came to my father
given by oracles, that he should die by the hand
of his son, how can you justly taunt me with that,
who then owned neither father's seed nor mother's womb,
but was a creature still unborn?
If then I appeared, as I did to my sorrow,
and came to blows with my father and murdered him,
knowing nothing of what I did, nor who he was,
how can you be right to blame that unknowing action?
For my mother's marriage, how can you be so shameless,
villain that you are, to make me speak of this?
She was your sister. But what that marriage was
I will say now. I will not hold my tongue,
when you have gone so far in impious speech.

She bore me, yes, she bore me—evil on evil—
she knowing no more than I did, and having borne me
brought forth, to her shame, those children to her son.
One thing I do know: *you* know what you do,
when you speak ill of her and me for this;
but when I married her *I* did not know
nor chose; nor, as I speak of it now,
do I choose willingly to speak.
Even in this marriage I will not be reviled,
nor accept the bitter blame of father-killer
with which you have belabored me incessantly.
Answer me only one of my questions—this one.
If someone here and now should stand beside you
trying to kill you—such a just man as you!—
would you ask the would-be killer was he your father,
or would you pay him back for the blow at once?
I think you would, if you love your life, pay back
the man who did it; you would not look around for justice.
Into such evil I entered, for the gods
guided me to it. I do not think
that my father's spirit, alive, would gainsay that.
But you, you are no just man—you think it right
to say everything, things not to be spoken,
as well as those proper to speech; you taunt me
before these people here. You speak flatteringly
of Theseus' glorious name.
You say how nobly Athens is administered.
With all your lavish praise you forget this:
that if there is a land that understands
how to worship the gods in honor, this land excels.
This is the city, I am the suppliant, old,
and you tried to steal me from it; you laid your hands
upon my daughters and made off with them.
For these your actions I call upon these Goddesses,
I beseech them, I entreat them with my prayers

to come as helpers and allies; so you shall learn
indeed what sort of government guards this city.

Chorus

My lord the stranger is a good man; what has happened to him
is all in all destructive; we should help him.

Theseus

We have talked enough; those who have done this deed
are hurrying away, while we the victims stand here.

Creon

What would you have me do? I am quite helpless.

Theseus

I want you to lead the way on their tracks, and I
must go as your escort; if you have these girls
still in my country, you may show them to me yourself.
If those who have them are in flight, we may spare our trouble,
for we have others to chase them. They will not escape
and fleeing from this country bless their gods for it!
Lead the way, you. Know, the taker is taken.
You were the hunter; Fortune has hunted you down.
What is gained by craft, unjustly, is not kept safely.
You need not look for anyone else to help you—
for I am sure that you were not alone
nor unprovided, seeing that you have reached
such recklessness and daring.
You must have some accomplice in whom you trusted.
I must look to all of this, nor make my city
weaker than a single man. Do you understand
anything of all this? Or are my words spoken in vain
as those were that were said to you when you planned this act?

Creon

I will not fault anything you say to me
when I am here. At home they will know what to do.

Theseus

Threaten—but go on! For you, Oedipus,
stay here at your ease, with absolute confidence
that if I do not die first, I will not rest
until I make your children yours again.

Oedipus

God bless you, Theseus, for your nobleness
and for the justice of your care for me!

Chorus

I would I were where the wheeling charge
of foemen soon will join
in fight to the clash of bronze,
on Pythian shores or the torch-lighted strand
where the Sacred Ones cherish
their solemn rites for mortal men,
on whose tongues the golden key rested
of the ministrant Eumolpidae.

There, I think, they shall reunite—
our Theseus, rouser of battles,
and the two captive sister maids,
in the midst of the warring of men strong to save,
still within Attic bounds.

But perhaps it is where they approach
the pastures of the west
of Oea's rock, snow-clad,
the prisoners riding or carried in chariots,
pushed to racing speed.

Creon will lose. Terrible is the might
of those that neighbor Colonus,
and terrible the might
of Theseus' folk.
Every bit shines, like a lightning flash.
Each horseman in eagerness rides,
with loosened bridle rein.

They are the horsemen who honor
Athene, goddess of horsemanship,
and the Sea Lord, Earth shaker,
dear son of Rhea.
Is the action started, or yet to come?
My mind gives me hints of hope
soon again to see the two girls
so cruelly tried,
so cruelly suffering
at the hands of their kinfolk.
Zeus will bring something to pass;
he will—and on this day.
I am the prophet
of happy outcome.
I would I were a dove in the sky,
quick of wing,
to reach a cloud over the fight
with eyes lifted above the fight.

O supreme ruler of Gods,
Zeus who sees everything,
grant that those who hold this land
may achieve triumph, may win the prize
with strength victorious.

Holy daughter of Zeus,
Pallas Athene, grant it,
and you Apollo, the hunter,
and your sister, the follower
of dappled deer. I beg you
for help to come doubly—
for this land and for its citizens.

Stranger and wanderer, you will not say
that I who watched on your behalf
was a false prophet. For I see
the girls returning here, and escorted, too.

Oedipus

Where? Where? What are you saying? How can it be?

Antigone

Father, O father! that some god would grant you
to sec this noble man who brought us home!

Oedipus

My dear, are you both here?

Antigone

Yes, for the hands
of Theseus and his dear servants rescued us.

Oedipus

Come to your father, child, and let me touch
that body I never hoped would come again!

Antigone

You shall have your wish. What you beg of us
is all our longing, too.

Oedipus

Where, oh where are you?

Antigone

Here, we are right beside you.

Oedipus

Dear children!

Antigone

All a father's love is there.

Oedipus

You loves, that have supported me!

Antigone

Poor daughters, and poor father!

Oedipus

I have what I love most. Were I still to die now,
I would not be wholly wretched,

for now I have you two beside me.
Press on me, you on this side, you on that,
clinging to your father; rest yourselves now
from all the old wandering, lonely and unhappy.
And tell me, but as shortly as you can
what has happened. For girls like you
a short tale suffices.

Antigone

Here is the man who rescued us. Hear him, father.
He did it all—so shall my telling
be brief enough.

Oedipus

Sir, do not wonder that with seeming obstinacy
I prolong this conversation with my children;
so utterly unexpected is what has happened!
But I know well that from none else than you
my joy in these has come to pass. You, you
it is that saved me, you and no other man.
May the gods grant all that I wish for you,
for you and for this country! Only in this people
of yours have I found piety towards the gods,
and human feeling and no hypocrisy.
I know all this—and with these words alone
do I requite what you have done. I have
all that I have through you and no one else.
My lord, reach me your right hand; let me touch it
and let me kiss your head—if that is lawful.

What am I saying? How can a wretched being,
such as I have become, wish to touch *you,*
a man in whom no single stain of evil
has dwelling place? I and you cannot do so.
Nor will I suffer it to be. The possibility
of sharing in my misery is only
for those already in it.
Stand where you are. God bless you where you stand!

In the days to come may you look after me
with the justice you have shown me in this hour!

Theseus

Even if you had extended your words longer,
I would not have wondered—for your delight in your children.
Nor would I, if you preferred their words to mine.
I have no weight of vexation at that.
I would have my life one of distinction,
not so much in words—rather by deeds achieved.
I let you see that what I swore to you
old man, I have not proved false to—not in anything.
For here I come, bringing your girls with me,
alive, untouched by all the threats against them.
How the fight was won, why should I boast pointlessly?
You yourself from these two will know all.

But there *is* something of question that has happened to me
as I came here; let me have your counsel on it.
It is little to tell, but remarkable. No man
should treat of anything as insignificant.

Oedipus

What is it, son of Aegeus? Tell me.
I do not know what it is you ask about.

Theseus

They say there is a man, no countryman
of yours, but of your kinfolk,
who had, it would seem, thrown himself down before
the altar of Poseidon, has taken his station there. It was
where I was sacrificing, when I came here to you.

Oedipus

What countryman is he? What does he want,
that he sits there as suppliant?

Theseus

I only know one thing.
He asks some little speech with you. This is no great matter.

Oedipus

What can it be? His suppliant seat there does not
suggest some trivial matter.

Theseus

What they say
is that he asks only to talk with you
and go away without suffering for coming here.

Oedipus

Who can he be that makes this supplication?

Theseus

Reflect if there be anyone in Argos
akin to you, that he might ask this favor.

Oedipus

Dearest of friends, stop right where you are!

Theseus

What is it?

Oedipus

Do not beg this of me.

Theseus

What is it, that I should not?

Oedipus

As I hear you, I know who this suppliant is.

Theseus

And who is he that I should find fault with him?

Oedipus

He is my son, prince, he is my hated son,
whose words would hurt my ears more than all others.

Theseus

What is this? Surely it's possible
to listen and not do what you do not want?
Why should it be so bitter to you to *hear* him?

Oedipus

His voice, prince, has become a thing most hateful
to me his father; do not constrain me
to yield in this.

Theseus

Consider if it be not his suppliancy
that makes your yielding a necessity.
Perhaps regard for the god should make you careful.

Antigone

Father, let me persuade you, though I am young to advise.
Suffer the king here to gratify his own heart
and give the god what the prince would have you give him.
For our sake *(pointing to her sister),* suffer our brother to come here.
He will not tear you from your resolution—
do not fear that—if he pleads what is unfit.
What harm is there in hearing what he says?
Evil contrivings are best revealed in speech.
You begot him; even if what he does to you
is the most impious of all that is vile,
you ought not, father, to match him in evil.
No, let him come. Other men have had bad sons,
and have had sharp tempers.
But when they were schooled by friends' enchanting voices
their natures yield to the might of them. You,
look to that other time—not now—
the father-and-mother evils that you suffered.
If you look at that other time, I am sure,
you will know the evil end of anger, the evil
which comes to climax in it. What your heart tells you then
are not slight things—when you lost those eyes, now sightless.
Yield to us all; it is not right
that those who ask what is just should have to be
importunate; nor that the man himself
who has had good treatment should not know how
to pay requital for it.

Oedipus

My child, when you win me with your words,
it is a bitter pleasure to yield. Let it be so,
as you will have it. Only, sir, if he comes here
let no one have the disposal of my life.

Theseus

Once is enough for that. I do not need to hear it twice,
old man; I do not want to boast, but you,
you know you are safe—if a god keeps *me* safe.

Chorus

Whoever it is that seeks to have
a greater share of life,
letting moderation slip out of his thoughts,
I count him a fool, a persistent fool;
I am clear in my mind of that.

Indeed, the long days store up many things
that are nearer to sorrow than joy,
and the whereabouts of delight
you will not find, once you have fallen
into the region beyond your due term.
The Helper still is the same for all,
the same Consummator,
Death at the last,
the appearance of Death in Doom.
He comes to no sound of wedding joy,
no lyre, no dances.

Not to be born is best of all;
when life is there, the second best
to go hence where you came,
with the best speed you may.
For when his youth with its gift of light heart
has come and gone, what grievous stroke
is spared to a man, what agony
is he without? Envy, and faction,

strife and fighting and murders are his,
and yet there is something more that claims him,
old age at the last, most hated,
without power, without comrades, and friends,
when every ill, all ills,
take up their dwelling with him.
So, he is old—this old man here—
I am not alone in that,
as the wave-lashed cape that faces north,
in the wintertime,
the din of the winds on every side,
the din of the mischiefs encompass him utterly,
like the breaking crests of the waves forever,
some from the setting sun,
some from his rising,
and some from the place of his midday beams,
and some from the northern mountains of night.

Antigone

Here he is, it seems, this stranger,
alone, my father, weeping his tears in floods,
as he comes here.

Oedipus

Who is it?

Antigone

He whom we always held in mind
that it would be; here is Polyneices.

Polyneices

O, what shall I do?
Shall I cry for my own troubles, first of all,
my sisters? Or his, my old father's,
as I see them before me?
Here I find him in a foreign country,
an exile banished here, with clothes upon him
where the foul ancient dirt has lived so long

that it infects his old body,
and his uncombed hair floats in the wind
about his eyeless face.
The food he carries to fill his belly,
is, I should guess, akin to what he wears.
I learn all this too late, wretch that I am!
I will bear witness against myself, as the world's villain,
for not supporting him. You need not learn
from others what I am.
But yet there is Mercy; in everything
she shares the throne of Zeus. Let her stand by you
too, father. Why are you silent?
Say something!
Do not turn away from me giving no answer,
sending me hence dishonored by your silence,
not even telling me why you are angry.
You children of this father, blood of my blood,
will you try at least to make him open his mouth
that now denies approach, in implacable silence?
So may he not dismiss me in dishonor—
a god's suppliant that I am—with never a word.

Antigone

Speak yourself, unhappy man, say what you come to seek.
The flood of words may give some kind of pleasure:
They may make angry or just bring some pity;
still, somehow, they give a voice to what is voiceless.

Polyneices

Then I will speak; your advice is good.
First, here I make the god my helper
from whose altar the prince of this country raised me up
to come to you. He granted me permission
to speak, and hear, and a safe-conduct home.
These things I would have from you, my foreign friends,
and from my sisters and my father.

Father, I want to tell you why I came here.
I have been banished from my country, made an exile,
because I claimed my right as the elder born
to sit upon your sovereign throne. For this,
my younger brother, Eteocles, drove me out.
He did not have the best of me in words,
nor in the proof of hand or deed. It was the city
which he persuaded. The chief reason, I think,
was the curse, *your* curse, that lay upon the house.
That is what I hear also from the soothsayers.

When I came to the Dorian land of Argos
Adrastus gave me his daughter to wife.
Then I swore to my side all
that were reputed best and honored most
for skill in warfare in the Apian land,
that I might gather from these a seven-fold band
of spearmen against Thebes; then with justice on my side
either die—or banish those that had done me wrong.
Very well, then; why have I come to you?
To bring, my father, my suppliant prayers, for myself
and for my allies, who with seven hosts
behind their seven spears encompass about
the entire plain of Thebes.

There is the spearman, Amphiareus, supreme
master in war, supreme in knowledge of omens;
the second is the Aetolian, son of Oeneus,
Tydeus; third Eteoclus, born an Argive;
the fourth Hippomedon, sent by his father Talaos;
the fifth Capaneus, who has vowed to burn
the city of Thebes into the ground; the sixth
Parthenopaeus, the Arcadian, hastens to the war,
his name recalling his mother, long a virgin
but brought at last to travail by the trusty
son of Atalanta;
and then myself, yours but not yours, begotten

of an evil fate, yet called at least your son,
I lead the fearless host of Argos to Thebes.

We all entreat you, by these your children, by
your life, my father, remit your heavy anger
against me, as I set forth to punish my brother
who thrust me out, despoiled me of my country.
For if there is any trust to be placed in oracles,
they have said the victory shall come to those
whose side you join.
Then, by our fountains, and our race's gods,
I beg you to be persuaded and to yield.
We are beggars and foreigners both—and so are you!
We live by flattering others, both you and I.
We have drawn the selfsame lot in life.
But he is a prince, at home—oh wretched me!—
and laughs at both of us, in luxury.
If you will stand a helper to my purpose
I will shake him out of it with little trouble
and quick enough, so that I can place you again
in your own house and place myself there too,
once I have driven him out and forcefully.
I may make this my boast if you stand by me,
without you I have no strength, even to survive.

Chorus

Oedipus, as to this man,
out of consideration for him that sent him here,
say what is proper and send him on his way.

Oedipus

Yes, public guardians of this land, I will.
If he that sent him to me had not been
Theseus, who thought it right that he should hear
words of mine, he never would have heard my voice.
But now he will go hence, having been thought worthy
and heard from me such words as never will
gladden his life.

You scoundrel, you, with your scepter and your throne—
held now by your blood brother in Thebes—
you chased me out, your father, made me cityless;
these are the clothes *you* made me wear,
the sight of which now brings tears to your eyes,
when *you* have come to the same stress of misery.
I may not weep, *I* must put up with it
as long as I live remembering my murderer;
you have contrived my rearing in agony;
you drove me out. It is because of you
I am a wanderer begging my daily bread.
Had I not begotten these children to be my nurses
I had been dead, for all you did to help.
Now it is they who save me, these very nurses.
They are men, not women, in bearing troubles with me.
You are no sons of mine, you are someone else's.
Therefore the Evil Spirit has eyes upon you,
although, by and by, those eyes will be still fiercer,
if these hosts are really moving towards Thebes.
That city you will not destroy—no, before that
you will fall yourself, polluted with blood, and equally
your brother. Such are the curses I sent forth
in days gone by, against you two. And now
I summon those curses to come to me as allies,
that you two, brothers, may know to reverence parents,
and not dishonor a father because he was blind—
and got such men as you for sons. These girls
have done none of this.
Therefore my curses overcome
your suppliant seat, and that, your throne, in Thebes,
as sure as Justice, claimed of old time, is sharer
in Zeus' throne, by the might of the old laws.
Get you gone! I spit you from me. I am no father
of yours, you worst of villains! Pack away
all of these curses that I invoke against you.
You shall not conquer by spear your native land;

you shall not come again to hollow Argos;
you are to die by a brother's hand, and kill him
by whom you were exiled.
There are my curses on you! And I summon
your father's hateful darkness of Tartarus
to give you a new dwelling place. I call
upon the spirits there, I call on Ares,
that thrust upon you both this dreadful hatred.

That is what you have heard. Now, off with you and tell
all the Cadmeans and your trusty allies
that such are the honors Oedipus divided
between those sons of his!

Chorus

I had no pleasure, Polyneices,
in your past journeyings. Now, speedily back again!

Polyneices

Woe for my journey! woe for its ill success!
Woe for my comrades! what an end this road had
when we set out from Argos! woe is me!
such an end that I cannot tell to any
of those comrades, nor yet turn *them* home again!
but, saying nothing, go on to meet my fortune.
Sisters—for you *are* my sisters, although his daughters—
since you have heard my father's dreadful curses,
I pray you two, by the gods, if the day come
when his curses come to pass, and you have somehow
come home again, do not dishonor me,
but lay me in a grave with funeral rites.
You have praise now, for the pains that you took,
in caring for this old man; you will earn no less
besides for helping me.

Antigone

Polyneices, I entreat you,
do the thing that I ask you.

Polyneices

Dearest Antigone,
what is it? Tell me.

Antigone

Turn your army
back to Argos speedily. Do not
destroy yourself and the city both.

Polyneices

I cannot
do this. How can I lead this selfsame army
back again when I have once
proved myself coward?

Antigone

Why must you, brother, fall to anger again?
If you destroy your own country, what do you gain?

Polyneices

Exile is shameful, and shameful that one elder
be so mocked by his brother.

Antigone

Do you see, then,
how right our father's prophecies come out
when he spoke of the mutual murder of you two?

Polyneices

That is what *he* wants. But I must not yield.

Antigone

Wretched that I am! But who, once he has heard
our father's prophecies, will dare to follow you?

Polyneices

I will not tell bad news. That is good generalship—
to tell one's strengths and not one's weaknesses.

Antigone

Then, brother, you are truly so determined?

Polyneices

Do not stop me. Now this must be my care,
this road of mine, ill-omened and terrible,
made so by my father and those Furies of his;
but may Zeus prosper *your* road, if you fulfill
my wishes, at my death. For me in life
there is nothing you can do. Let me go now,
and, both of you, goodbye. You will never again
see me alive.

Antigone

My heart is broken!

Polyneices

Do not mourn for me.

Antigone

Brother, how can anyone
not mourn, seeing you set out
to death so clear before you?

Polyneices

If die I must, I'll die.

Antigone

Do not, dearest;
do as I say.

Polyneices

Do not try to persuade me
to fail my duty.

Antigone

Then I am utterly
destroyed if I must lose you.

Polyneices

All of that
whether for good or ill, Fortune determines.
But for you two, I pray the gods that never

you meet with ill. In all men's judgment
you should not suffer misfortune.

Chorus

Here are other new ills that have come
just now, of evil doom,
from the blind stranger—
unless Fate is somehow at work.
For I cannot call any decision of God
a vain thing.
Time watches constantly those decisions;
Some fortunes it destroys, and others,
on the day following, lifts up again.

There is the thunder! Zeus!

Oedipus

My children, children, please can someone go
and fetch for me Theseus that best of men?

Antigone

Father, what is the occasion of your summons?

Oedipus

The winged thunder of Zeus will carry me
straightway to death. Send and send quickly!

Chorus

Look at it! rolling down, crashing,
the thunderbolt unspeakable, hurled by Zeus.
Terror has raised the hair on my head;
my heart is trembling.
There, again, is the flash of the lightning!
It burns in the sky. What event will it yield?
I am all fear. It is not for nothing
when it lightens so; there will be issue of it.
O, the great sky! O Zeus!

Oedipus

Children, there has come to me, as the gods said,
my end of life. There is no more turning away.

Antigone

How do you know? What makes you think it?

Oedipus

I know it well. But, quickly, someone go
and summon here this country's prince.

Chorus

See, there again, around us
the piercing thunder!
Be merciful, God, if you are bringing
some black-night thing
to this land, our mother.
May I find you gracious.
Because I have looked on a man accursed
may I not have a share in a graceless grace!
Lord Zeus, to you I cry.

Oedipus

Is the man near? And children, will he find me
still alive and my wits not astray?

Antigone

What confidence would you implant in his mind?

Oedipus

That, for the kindness he has shown me, the requital,
as I once promised, now is duly paid.

Chorus

My son, come here,
or if in the innermost recess of the glade
you are hallowing Poseidon's altar
with sacrifice of cattle, come still.
For the stranger claims to make return
to you, and the city and his friends,
a just return for a just kindness done.

Theseus

What is this public summons from all of you,
clearly from my people, clearly from this stranger?

Is it the thunder of Zeus or rushing hail?
One can indeed conjecture anything
when Zeus sends such a storm.

Oedipus

My lord, I have longed for you and you have come.
Some god has made for you a happy blessing
from this coming.

Theseus

What new thing is it, son of Laius?

Oedipus

The balance of my life's scale has come down.
I will not choose to fail my promises
to you and the city, now, before I die.

Theseus

What evidence have you of this impending death?

Oedipus

The gods are their own messengers to me;
they are not false to the signs they have arranged.

Theseus

What signs? Make this clear, old man.

Oedipus

The long continued thunder, the massive lightning
hurled from the hand that never knew defeat.

Theseus

I believe you; for I have seen you prophesy
much, and falsely never. Tell me what to do.

Oedipus

Yes; I will direct you, son of Aegeus,
in what shall be a treasure for this city.
Old age shall not decay it. Immediately
I will show the way without a hand to guide me
to the place where I must die.
And you, describe this to no man, ever,

neither where it is hidden nor in what region,
that doing so may make you a defense
beyond the worth of many shields, or many neighbors' help.
The things within this ban, not to be uttered,
yourself shall learn, when you come there alone,
for I shall not declare them to anyone
of these citizens, nor to my daughters, dear though I hold them.
Keep them yourself always, and when you come
to the end of life reveal them only
to him that is nearest to you, and he in turn
to his successor.
So you shall hold this city undevastated
by the Sown Men. Ten thousand states
have committed violence on one another,
despite their rulers' excellent government.
For the gods are careful watchers at the last
but slow in action, when one dismissing gods' will
has turned to madness. Never
let that befall you, son of Aegeus.
But I will not school you in such things; you know them.
Let us now go to the place—a pressing summons
from the god forces me—and delay no more.
My children, follow me—so. In a strange way
I have become your guide; you were once mine.
Come on, but touch me not. Suffer me to find
my sacred grave where it is fated
that I shall be hidden in this country's earth.
This way, this way, like this! For this way Hermes,
the Conductor, leads me, and the goddess of the dead.
O light, no light though you were once a light
to me! now for the last time touch my body.
For I creep along to hide my last of life
in Hades. You dearest of friends *(to Theseus)*
yourself, this land and these your citizens—
blessings upon you! and in your blessedness
remember me, the dead! Live blessed forever.

Chorus

If it be lawful, it is mine
to adore with prayers the Goddess Unseen
and you, my lord of the Creatures of Night,
Aidoneus, Aidoneus,
that our stranger friend may pass to his end
untroubled and free of the tears
attendant on a grievous doom;
that he may come to the world below,
that hides all within itself,
to the land of the dead, the Stygian house.
Many the ills that were his, all uncalled for;
may God in justice exalt him again!

O goddesses of that Underworld,
and Form of the Hound Unconquered
who keeps his lair at the guest-haunted gate,
and sleeps and snuffles from out his cave,
the guardian in death's house, unsubdued—
thus is always the story told.

O son of Earth and Tartarus
I pray that that Hound may give a clear path
to our friend coming down
to dead men's country;
You, Giver of Sleep Everlasting,
I call on You.

Messenger

Citizens: to speak most briefly and truthfully,
Oedipus is gone. But what has happened,
the tale of that cannot be told so briefly,
for the acts there were not brief.

Chorus

The unhappy man is gone!

Messenger

You must think of him
as of one truly parted out of life.

Chorus

How was it? By God's chance and painlessly
the poor man ended?

Messenger

That is wonderful indeed.
How he moved from here with no guidance of friends,
you yourselves know. For I think you were here.
He was himself the guide to all of us.
When he came to the steep road, rooted in earth
by brazen steps, he stood in one of the many
branching paths, near the hollow basin
where is, forever confident, the memorial
to Theseus' and Peirithous' compact.
Where he stood, he was midway between
that basin and the Thorician rock,
the hollow pear tree and the grave of stone.

Then he sat down and loosed his filthy robes,
cried loudly to his daughters to bring him water
from some stream, to wash and make drink offerings.
They hurried to Demeter's hill, in front of them,
guardian of tender plants; they brought what he ordered;
and then with lustral washing and with clothes
equipped him in the customary fashion.
When he had his pleasure of all he did,
and nothing that he sought was scanted, Zeus
of the Underworld thundered. They fell at their father's knees
and cried, ceaselessly, beating their breasts,
and with unending long laments. But he,
when he heard the sudden bitter cries from them,
folded his hands upon them; then said "My children,
this is the day when you become fatherless.
All that was me has perished; now no more

for you the heavy task of tending me.
It was a cruel task, children, that I know,
but there's a single word that overthrows
all tasks of work. My love you had; no one
could love you more. That is the love you lose now
and must pass through the rest of life without it."
They embraced and sobbed shrilly, all three of them.
When they came to the end of their mourning
and not another cry rose, there, in the stillness,
there was a voice of someone, summoning him,
and suddenly in their terror, all hair stood up.
It was the god who called him, over and over,
"You, Oedipus, Oedipus, why are you hesitating
to go our way? You have been too slow, too long."
When he understood that calling of the god,
he cried to this country's ruler, Theseus,
to come to him, and when he came, he said:
"You that I love, give me your hand's sworn pledge
to these my children, and you, my children, to him.
Promise me that you will never consciously
forsake them, but perform whatever you judge
will be for their advantage always."
He, noble man that he is, gave him his promise
and with no word of sorrow swore he would do
that, for his friend.
When he had finished, suddenly Oedipus
touching his children with blind hands said "Both, my children,
be brave and noble of mind, and leave this place.
Do not seek to know what is forbidden,
nor hear it from others' speaking.
Quickly, away with you; only let Theseus
stay to understand what is to be done."

That was what he said; we listened all,
and with the girls in tears and lamentations,
followed them away. When we departed,

in a few moments we looked back and saw that
Oedipus, yes, Oedipus, was no longer there,
but the king by himself, holding his hand
before his face, to shade his eyes, as though
some deadly terror had appeared to him
that sight could not endure.
Then just a little afterwards, we saw him
bow to salute the earth and the gods' Olympus
united in the same prayer at once.
But by what manner of doom that other died
no mortal man can say, save our lord Theseus.
It was no fiery thunderbolt of God
that made away with him, nor a sea hurricane
rising; no, it was some messenger
sent by the gods, or some power of the dead
split open the fundament of earth, with good will,
to give him painless entry. He was sent on his way
with no accompaniment of tears, no pain of sickness;
if any man ended miraculously,
this man did. If I seem to talk nonsense,
I would not try to win over such as think so.

Chorus

Where are the girls? And where their escorting friends?

Messenger

Not far away. The sounds of their mourning voices
show they are coming here.

Antigone

Now it belongs to both of us,
unhappy beings, to sorrow
for the curse that inheres
in our father's blood;
not for this part, yes, and for that part, no—
totally.
For him we have borne in his life
a great burden unrelieved,

but now at the end we will have to speak
of things beyond reason's scope,
what we saw, what we suffered.

Chorus

What is it?

Antigone

My friends, we can only guess.

Chorus

He has gone?

Antigone

As you would have him go.
What else can be said of one
whom neither the War God,
nor the sea encountered,
but the unseen fields of the world of Death
snatched away in some doom invisible?
On us two destruction's night
has settled on our eyes.
How shall we wander, how find
a bitter living in distant lands
or on the waves of the sea?

Ismene

I do not know.
Let murdering Hades
take me and join me in death with him,
my father in his old age.
The life that will henceforth be mine
is a life that cannot be lived.

Chorus

You two are the best of children;
you must bear what the god gives to bear.
No more fire of grief. You cannot truly
sorrow for what has happened.

Antigone

There can be a love
even of suffering;
for that which is anything but dear itself
could still be dear,
while I still had him in these hands of mine.
Father, dear one, you that forever
have put on the darkness of underground,
even there you shall not be unloved,
by me and by my sister.

Chorus

His end?

Antigone

His end is what he wished.

Chorus

What end?

Antigone

And he died in a foreign land,
but one he yearned for. He has his bed
below in the shadowy grass
forever.
He has left behind him a mourning sorrow—
these eyes of mine with their tears
bewail you. I do not know how
in my misery I should cast out
such a weight of sorrow.
Yes, you chose in a foreign land
to die. I find it a lonely death.

Ismene

What further destiny awaits
you and me, dear one, alone as we are?

Chorus

My dears, the end of his life was blessed;
do not keep sorrowing. No one
is hard for misfortune to capture.

Antigone

Let us hurry back, sister.

Ismene

What to do?

Antigone

Desire possesses me—

Ismene

What desire?

Antigone

To see where he lies in earth.

Ismene

Who lies?

Antigone

Our father—Oh, misery!

Ismene

How can that be lawful?
Do you not see?

Antigone

Why do you blame me for this?

Ismene

And this again—

Antigone

What is *this* again?

Ismene

Where he fell, there *is* no grave—
and he was quite alone.

Antigone
Bring me where he was,
and then kill me.

Ismene
Where now so lonely,
so helpless, shall *I* live?

Chorus
Friends, do not be afraid!

Antigone
But where to find refuge?

Chorus
You *have* found refuge.

Antigone
From what?

Chorus
From misfortune, refuge for you both.

Antigone
I understand.

Chorus
What is it you are thinking?

Antigone
I cannot tell
how I can come home.

Chorus
Do not seek to go home.

Antigone
Trouble is upon us.

Chorus
It has pursued you before.

Antigone
Desperate then, but now still worse.

Chorus

Yes, yours was a sea of sorrow.

Antigone

Where shall we go, O God?
To what of hope now
can Fate drive us?

(Theseus enters.)

Theseus

Cease your mourning, children; for those
to whom the grace of the Underworld Gods
has been stored as a treasure, to the quick and the dead,
for them there shall be no mourning.
Else the gods may be angry.

Antigone

Son of Aegeus, we beg you—

Theseus

What would you have me grant, children?

Antigone

We would ourselves see the grave
of our father.

Theseus

No, this is not lawful.

Antigone

What do you mean, king of Athens?

Theseus

He
has forbidden approach to the place,
nor may any voice invoke
the sacred tomb where he lies.
He said, if I truly did this,
I should have forever a land unharmed.

These pledges the God heard from me
and Oath, Zeus' servant, all seeing.

Antigone

If this was, then, the mind of Him,
the dead, I must be content.
Send us, then, to our ancient Thebes
that perhaps we may prevent
the murder that comes to our brothers.

Theseus

That I will do and whatever else
shall profit yourselves and pleasure both you
and the man under earth who is newly gone—
for him I must spare no pains.

Chorus

Now cease lamentation, nor further prolong
your dirge. All of these matters
have found their consummation.

THE BACCHAE

Translated by William Arrowsmith

INTRODUCTION

Euripides wrote *The Bacchae* in the last years of his life during a self-imposed exile in Macedon. It was produced in Athens after his death, which occurred in 406 B.C., and won a posthumous first prize.

Dionysus himself speaks a most explicit prologue, setting forth the facts of his case, and the action proceeds from this point along clearly drawn lines. The reader needs no summary. But a few comments may help. Dionysus, on stage as a mortal, is a new god fighting for recognition as a god in the city of his birth, which should be the first to recognize him and has rejected him. If he is the acknowledged son of Zeus and Semele, he would be at least heroic; in this case he is divine. If Zeus is not his father, he is a bastard foundling and an impostor. Through madness and slaughter he punishes his doubting kinsmen and is established as a god at the end.

The actual drama is played out as a struggle between two young men, Dionysus and his cousin Pentheus, master of Thebes. Above and beyond the individuals, even the god, is what Dionysus stands for, not wine only, but a new kind of religion. Accepted, it means pious devotion; resisted, it will still force its way in, as madness. The devout Bacchae of the Chorus have accepted; the mad women in the hills have had Bacchism forced on them. Pentheus is defeated by invasion from within, and his integrity has surrendered to the power of Dionysus before he goes to his death. The utterances of the Chorus constantly go beyond the immediate issues of the action, to celebrate a new religious feeling, open to the will of all human beings, barbarians as well as Hellenes, the weak, poor, and unlettered as well as the strong, rich, and wise. These choral odes, the wildest and most original to be found in Euripides, do somewhat to relieve the horrors in a story of vengeance and brutal punishment.

NOTE

The text of this translation is the Oxford text of Gilbert Murray, supplemented by the brilliant commentary of E. R. Dodds.

CHARACTERS

Dionysus (also called Bromius, Evius, and Bacchus)

Chorus of Asian Bacchae (followers of Dionysus)

Teiresias

Cadmus

Pentheus

Attendant

First Messenger

Second Messenger

Agave

Coryphaeus (chorus leader)

For Anne and George
ex voto
XAIPETE

THE BACCHAE

SCENE: *Before the royal palace at Thebes. On the left is the way to Cithaeron; on the right, to the city. In the center of the orchestra stands, still smoking, the vine-covered tomb of Semele, mother of Dionysus.*

Enter Dionysus. He is of soft, even effeminate, appearance. His face is beardless; he is dressed in a fawn-skin and carries a thyrsus (i.e., a stalk of fennel tipped with ivy leaves). On his head he wears a wreath of ivy, and his long blond curls ripple down over his shoulders. Throughout the play he wears a smiling mask.

Dionysus

I am Dionysus, the son of Zeus,
come back to Thebes, this land where I was born.
My mother was Cadmus' daughter, Semele by name,
midwived by fire, delivered by the lightning's
blast.
And here I stand, a god incognito,
disguised as man, beside the stream of Dirce
and the waters of Ismenus. There before the palace
I see my lightning-married mother's grave,
and there upon the ruins of her shattered house
the living fire of Zeus still smolders on
in deathless witness of Hera's violence and rage
against my mother. But Cadmus wins my praise:
he has made this tomb a shrine, sacred to my mother.
It was I who screened her grave with the green
of the clustering vine.
Far behind me lie
those golden-rivered lands, Lydia and Phrygia,
where my journeying began. Overland I went,
across the steppes of Persia where the sun strikes hotly
down, through Bactrian fastness and the grim waste
of Media. Thence to rich Arabia I came;

and so, along all Asia's swarming littoral
of towered cities where Greeks and foreign nations,
mingling, live, my progress made. There
I taught my dances to the feet of living men,
establishing my mysteries and rites
that I might be revealed on earth for what I am:
a god.
      And thence to Thebes.
                              This city, first
in Hellas, now shrills and echoes to my women's cries,
their ecstasy of joy. Here in Thebes
I bound the fawn-skin to the women's flesh and armed
their hands with shafts of ivy. For I have come
to refute that slander spoken by my mother's sisters—
those who least had right to slander her.
They said that Dionysus was no son of Zeus,
but Semele had slept beside a man in love
and fathered off her shame on Zeus—a fraud, they sneered,
contrived by Cadmus to protect his daughter's name.
They said she lied, and Zeus in anger at that lie
blasted her with lightning.
                              Because of that offense
I have stung them with frenzy, hounded them from home
up to the mountains where they wander, crazed of mind,
and compelled to wear my orgies' livery.
Every woman in Thebes—but the women only—
I drove from home, mad. There they sit,
rich and poor alike, even the daughters of Cadmus,
beneath the silver firs on the roofless rocks.
Like it or not, this city must learn its lesson:
it lacks initiation in my mysteries;
that I shall vindicate my mother Semele
and stand revealed to mortal eyes as the god
she bore to Zeus.
                  Cadmus the king has abdicated,
leaving his throne and power to his grandson Pentheus;

who now revolts against divinity, in *me;*
thrusts *me* from his offerings; forgets *my* name
in his prayers. Therefore I shall *prove* to him
and every man in Thebes that I am god
indeed. And when my worship is established here,
and all is well, then I shall go my way
and be revealed to other men in other lands.
But if the men of Thebes attempt to force
my Bacchae from the mountainside by threat of arms,
I shall marshal my Maenads and take the field.
To these ends I have laid my deity aside
and go disguised as man.

(He wheels and calls offstage.)

On, my women,
women who worship me, women whom I led
out of Asia where Tmolus heaves its rampart
over Lydia!
On, comrades of my progress here!
Come, and with your native Phrygian drum—
Rhea's drum and mine—pound at the palace doors
of Pentheus! Let the city of Thebes behold you,
while I return among Cithaeron's forest glens
where my Bacchae wait and join their whirling dances.

(Exit Dionysus as the Chorus of Asian Bacchae comes dancing in from the right. They are dressed in fawn-skins, crowned with ivy, and carry thyrsi, timbrels, and flutes.)

Chorus

Out of the land of Asia,
down from holy Tmolus,
speeding the service of god,
for Bromius we come!
Hard are the labors of god;
hard, but his service is sweet.
Sweet to serve, sweet to cry:
Bacchus! *Evohé!*

—You on the streets!
—You on the roads!
—Make way!
—Let every mouth be hushed. Let no ill-omened words
profane your tongues.
—Make way! Fall back!
—Hush.
—For now I raise the old, old hymn to Dionysus.

—Blessèd, blessèd are those who know the mysteries of god.
—Blessèd is he who hallows his life in the worship of god,
he whom the spirit of god possesseth, who is one
with those who belong to the holy body of god.
—Blessèd are the dancers and those who are purified,
who dance on the hill in the holy dance of god.
—Blessèd are they who keep the rite of Cybele the Mother.
—Blessèd are the thyrsus-bearers, those who wield in their hands
the holy wand of god.
—Blessèd are those who wear the crown of the ivy of god.
—Blessèd, blessèd are they: Dionysus is their god!

—On, Bacchae, on, you Bacchae,
bear your god in triumph home!
Bear on the god, son of god,
escort your Dionysus home!
Bear him down from Phrygian hill,
attend him through the streets of Hellas!

—So his mother bore him once
in labor bitter; lightning-struck,
forced by fire that flared from Zeus,
consumed, she died, untimely torn,
in childbed dead by blow of light!
Of light the son was born!

—Zeus it was who saved his son;
with speed outrunning mortal eye,

bore him to a private place,
bound the boy with clasps of gold;
in his thigh as in a womb,
concealed his son from Hera's eyes.

—And when the weaving Fates fulfilled the time,
the bull-horned god was born of Zeus. In joy
he crowned his son, set serpents on his head—
wherefrom, in piety, descends to us
the Maenad's writhing crown, her *chevelure* of snakes.

—O Thebes, nurse of Semele,
crown your hair with ivy!
Grow green with bryony!
Redden with berries! O city,
with boughs of oak and fir,
come dance the dance of god!
Fringe your skins of dappled fawn
with tufts of twisted wool!
Handle with holy care
the violent wand of god!
And let the dance begin!
He is Bromius who runs
to the mountain!
to the mountain!
where the throng of women waits,
driven from shuttle and loom,
possessed by Dionysus!

—And I praise the holies of Crete,
the caves of the dancing Curetes,
there where Zeus was born,
where helmed in triple tier
around the primal drum
the Corybantes danced. They,
they were the first of all
whose whirling feet kept time

to the strict beat of the taut hide
and the squeal of the wailing flute.
Then from them to Rhea's hands
the holy drum was handed down;
but, stolen by the raving Satyrs,
fell at last to me and now
accompanies the dance
which every other year
celebrates your name:
Dionysus!

—He is sweet upon the mountains. He drops to the earth
from the running packs.
He wears the holy fawn-skin. He hunts the wild goat
and kills it.
He delights in the raw flesh.
He runs to the mountains of Phrygia, to the mountains
of Lydia he runs!
He is Bromius who leads us! *Evohé!*

—With milk the earth flows! It flows with wine!
It runs with the nectar of bees!

—Like frankincense in its fragrance
is the blaze of the torch he bears.
Flames float out from his trailing wand
as he runs, as he dances,
kindling the stragglers,
spurring with cries,
and his long curls stream to the wind!

—And he cries, as they cry, *Evohé!*—
On, Bacchae!
On, Bacchae!
Follow, glory of golden Tmolus,
hymning god
with a rumble of drums,

with a cry, *Evohé!* to the Evian god,
with a cry of Phrygian cries,
when the holy flute like honey plays
the sacred song of those who go
to the mountain!
to the mountain!

—Then, in ecstasy, like a colt by its grazing mother,
the Bacchante runs with flying feet, she leaps!

(The Chorus remains grouped in two semicircles about the orchestra as Teiresias makes his entrance. He is incongruously dressed in the bacchant's fawn-skin and is crowned with ivy. Old and blind, he uses his thyrsus to tap his way.)

Teiresias

Ho there, who keeps the gates?
Summon Cadmus—
Cadmus, Agenor's son, the stranger from Sidon
who built the towers of our Thebes.
Go, someone.
Say Teiresias wants him. He will know what errand
brings me, that agreement, age with age, we made
to deck our wands, to dress in skins of fawn
and crown our heads with ivy.

(Enter Cadmus from the palace. Dressed in Dionysiac costume and bent almost double with age, he is an incongruous and pathetic figure.)

Cadmus

My old friend,
I knew it must be you when I heard your summons.
For there's a wisdom in his voice that makes
the man of wisdom known.
But here I am,
dressed in the costume of the god, prepared to go.
Insofar as we are able, Teiresias, we must

do honor to this god, for he was born
my daughter's son, who has been revealed to men,
the god, Dionysus.
Where shall we go, where
shall we tread the dance, tossing our white heads
in the dances of god?
Expound to me, Teiresias.
For in such matters you are wise.
Surely
I could dance night and day, untiringly
beating the earth with my thyrsus! And how sweet it is
to forget my old age.

Teiresias

It is the same with me.
I too feel young, young enough to dance.

Cadmus

Good. Shall we take our chariots to the mountain?

Teiresias

Walking would be better. It shows more honor
to the god.

Cadmus

So be it. I shall lead, my old age
conducting yours.

Teiresias

The god will guide us there
with no effort on our part.

Cadmus

Are we the only men
who will dance for Bacchus?

Teiresias

They are all blind.
Only we can see.

Cadmus

But we delay too long.
Here, take my arm.

Teiresias

Link my hand in yours.

Cadmus

I am a man, nothing more. I do not scoff
at heaven.

Teiresias

We do not trifle with divinity.
No, we are the heirs of customs and traditions
hallowed by age and handed down to us
by our fathers. No quibbling logic can topple *them*,
whatever subtleties this clever age invents.
People may say: "Aren't you ashamed? At your age,
going dancing, wreathing your head with ivy?"
Well, I am *not* ashamed. Did the god declare
that just the young or just the old should dance?
No, he desires his honor from all mankind.
He wants no one excluded from his worship.

Cadmus

Because you cannot see, Teiresias, let me be
interpreter for you this once. Here comes
the man to whom I left my throne, Echion's son,
Pentheus, hastening toward the palace. He seems
excited and disturbed. Yes, listen to him.

(Enter Pentheus from the right. He is a young man of athletic build, dressed in traditional Greek dress; like Dionysus, he is beardless. He enters excitedly, talking to the attendants who accompany him.)

Pentheus

I happened to be away, out of the city,
but reports reached me of some strange mischief here,

stories of our women leaving home to frisk
in mock ecstasies among the thickets on the mountain,
dancing in honor of the latest divinity,
a certain Dionysus, whoever he may be!
In their midst stand bowls brimming with wine.
And then, one by one, the women wander off
to hidden nooks where they serve the lusts of men.
Priestesses of Bacchus they claim they are,
but it's really Aphrodite they adore.
I have captured some of them; my jailers
have locked them away in the safety of our prison.
Those who run at large shall be hunted down
out of the mountains like the animals they are—
yes, my own mother Agave, and Ino
and Autonoë, the mother of Actaeon.
In no time at all I shall have them trapped
in iron nets and stop this obscene disorder.
  I am also told a foreigner has come to Thebes
from Lydia, one of those charlatan magicians,
with long yellow curls smelling of perfumes,
with flushed cheeks and the spells of Aphrodite
in his eyes. His days and nights he spends
with women and girls, dangling before them the joys
of initiation in his mysteries.
But let me bring him underneath that roof
and I'll stop his pounding with his wand and tossing
his head. By god, I'll have his head cut off!
And *this* is the man who claims that Dionysus
is a god and was sewn into the thigh of Zeus,
when, in point of fact, that same blast of lightning
consumed him and his mother both for her lie
that she had lain with Zeus in love. Whoever
this stranger is, aren't such impostures,
such unruliness, worthy of hanging?

(For the first time he sees Teiresias and Cadmus in their Dionysiac costumes.)

What!
But this is incredible! Teiresias the seer
tricked out in a dappled fawn-skin!
And *you*,
you, my own grandfather, playing at the bacchant
with a wand!
Sir, I shrink to see your old age
so foolish. Shake that ivy off, grandfather!
Now drop that wand. Drop it, I say.
(*He wheels on Teiresias.*)
Aha,
I see: this is *your* doing, Teiresias.
Yes, you want still another god revealed to men
so you can pocket the profits from burnt offerings
and bird-watching. By heaven, only your age
restrains me now from sending you to prison
with those Bacchic women for importing here to Thebes
these filthy mysteries. When once you see
the glint of wine shining at the feasts of women,
then you may be sure the festival is rotten.

Coryphaeus

What blasphemy! Stranger, have you no respect
for heaven? For Cadmus who sowed the dragon teeth?
Will the son of Echion disgrace his house?

Teiresias

Give a wise man an honest brief to plead
and his eloquence is no remarkable achievement.
But you are glib; your phrases come rolling out
smoothly on the tongue, as though your words were wise
instead of foolish. The man whose glibness flows
from his conceit of speech declares the thing he is:
a worthless and a stupid citizen.
I tell you,
this god whom you ridicule shall someday have

enormous power and prestige throughout Hellas.
Mankind, young man, possesses two supreme blessings.
First of these is the goddess Demeter, or Earth—
whichever name you choose to call her by.
It was she who gave to man his nourishment of grain.
But after her there came the son of Semele,
who matched her present by inventing liquid wine
as his gift to man. For filled with that good gift,
suffering mankind forgets its grief; from it
comes sleep; with it oblivion of the troubles
of the day. There is no other medicine
for misery. And when we pour libations
to the gods, we pour the god of wine himself
that through his intercession man may win
the favor of heaven.

You sneer, do you, at that story
that Dionysus was sewed into the thigh of Zeus?
Let me teach you what that really means. When Zeus
rescued from the thunderbolt his infant son,
he brought him to Olympus. Hera, however,
plotted at heart to hurl the child from heaven.
Like the god he is, Zeus countered her. Breaking off
a tiny fragment of that ether which surrounds the world,
he molded from it a dummy Dionysus.
This he *showed* to Hera, but with time men garbled
the word and said that Dionysus had been *sewed*
into the thigh of Zeus. This was their story,
whereas, in fact, Zeus *showed* the dummy to Hera
and gave it as a hostage for his son.

Moreover,
this is a god of prophecy. His worshippers,
like madmen, are endowed with mantic powers.
For when the god enters the body of a man
he fills him with the breath of prophecy.

Besides,

he has usurped even the functions of warlike Ares.
Thus, at times, you see an army mustered under arms
stricken with panic before it lifts a spear.
This panic comes from Dionysus.
Someday
you shall even see him bounding with his torches
among the crags at Delphi, leaping the pastures
that stretch between the peaks, whirling and waving
his thyrsus: great throughout Hellas.
Mark my words,
Pentheus. Do not be so certain that power
is what matters in the life of man; do not mistake
for wisdom the fantasies of your sick mind.
Welcome the god to Thebes; crown your head;
pour him libations and join his revels.
Dionysus does not, I admit, *compel* a woman
to be chaste. Always and in every case
it is her character and nature that keeps
a woman chaste. But even in the rites of Dionysus,
the chaste woman will not be corrupted.
Think:
you are pleased when men stand outside your doors
and the city glorifies the name of Pentheus.
And so the god: he too delights in glory.
But Cadmus and I, whom you ridicule, will crown
our heads with ivy and join the dances of the god—
an ancient foolish pair perhaps, but dance
we must. Nothing you have said would make me
change my mind or flout the will of heaven.
You are mad, grievously mad, beyond the power
of any drugs to cure, for you are drugged
with madness.

Coryphaeus

Apollo would approve your words.
Wisely you honor Bromius: a great god.

Cadmus

My boy,
Teiresias advises well. Your home is here
with us, with our customs and traditions, not
outside, alone. Your mind is distracted now,
and what you think is sheer delirium.
Even if this Dionysus is no god,
as you assert, persuade yourself that he is.
The fiction is a noble one, for Semele will seem
to be the mother of a god, and this confers
no small distinction on our family.
You saw
that dreadful death your cousin Actaeon died
when those man-eating hounds he had raised himself
savaged him and tore his body limb from limb
because he boasted that his prowess in the hunt surpassed
the skill of Artemis.
Do not let his fate be yours.
Here, let me wreathe your head with leaves of ivy.
Then come with us and glorify the god.

Pentheus

Take your hands off me! Go worship your Bacchus,
but do not wipe your madness off on me.
By god, I'll make him pay, the man who taught you
this folly of yours.

(*He turns to his attendants.*)

Go, someone, this instant,
to the place where this prophet prophesies.
Pry it up with crowbars, heave it over,
upside down; demolish everything you see.
Throw his fillets out to wind and weather.
That will provoke him more than anything.
As for the rest of you, go and scour the city
for that effeminate stranger, the man who infects our women
with this strange disease and pollutes our beds.

And when you take him, clap him in chains
and march him here. He shall die as he deserves—
by being stoned to death. He shall come to rue
his merrymaking here in Thebes.

(*Exeunt attendants.*)

Teiresias

Reckless fool,
you do not know the consequences of your words.
You talked madness before, but this is raving
lunacy!
Cadmus, let us go and pray
for this raving fool and for this city too,
pray to the god that no awful vengeance strike
from heaven.
Take your staff and follow me.
Support me with your hands, and I shall help you too
lest we stumble and fall, a sight of shame,
two old men together.
But go we must,
acknowledging the service that we owe to god,
Bacchus, the son of Zeus.
And yet take care
lest someday your house repent of Pentheus
in its sufferings. I speak not prophecy
but fact. The words of fools finish in folly.

(*Exeunt Teiresias and Cadmus. Pentheus retires into the palace.*)

Chorus

—Holiness, queen of heaven,
Holiness on golden wing
who hover over earth,
do you hear what Pentheus says?
Do you hear his blasphemy
against the prince of the blessèd,
the god of garlands and banquets,

Bromius, Semele's son?
These blessings he gave:
laughter to the flute
and the loosing of cares
when the shining wine is spilled
at the feast of the gods,
and the wine-bowl casts its sleep
on feasters crowned with ivy.

—A tongue without reins,
defiance, unwisdom—
their end is disaster.
But the life of quiet good,
the wisdom that accepts—
these abide unshaken,
preserving, sustaining
the houses of men.
Far in the air of heaven,
the sons of heaven live.
But they watch the lives of men.
And what passes for wisdom is not;
unwise are those who aspire,
who outrange the limits of man.
Briefly, we live. Briefly,
then die. Wherefore, I say,
he who hunts a glory, he who tracks
some boundless, superhuman dream,
may lose his harvest here and now
and garner death. Such men are mad,
their counsels evil.

—O let me come to Cyprus,
island of Aphrodite,
homes of the loves that cast
their spells on the hearts of men!
Or Paphos where the hundred-
mouthed barbarian river

brings ripeness without rain!
To Pieria, haunt of the Muses,
and the holy hill of Olympus!
O Bromius, leader, god of joy,
Bromius, take me there!
There the lovely Graces go,
and there Desire, and there
the right is mine to worship
as I please.

—The deity, the son of Zeus,
in feast, in festival, delights.
He loves the goddess Peace,
generous of good,
preserver of the young.
To rich and poor he gives
the simple gift of wine,
the gladness of the grape.
But him who scoffs he hates,
and him who mocks his life,
the happiness of those
for whom the day is blessed
but doubly blessed the night;
whose simple wisdom shuns the thoughts
of proud, uncommon men and all
their god-encroaching dreams.
But what the common people do,
the things that simple men believe,
I too believe and do.

(As Penthus reappears from the palace, enter from the left several attendants leading Dionysus captive.)

Attendant

Pentheus, here we are; not empty-handed either.
We captured the quarry you sent us out to catch.
But our prey here was tame: refused to run

or hide, held out his hands as willing as you please,
completely unafraid. His ruddy cheeks were flushed
as though with wine, and he stood there smiling,
making no objection when we roped his hands
and marched him here. It made me feel ashamed.
"Listen, stranger," I said, "I am not to blame.
We act under orders from Pentheus. He ordered
your arrest."
As for those women you clapped in chains
and sent to the dungeon, they're gone, clean away,
went skipping off to the fields crying on their god
Bromius. The chains on their legs snapped apart
by themselves. Untouched by any human hand,
the doors swung wide, opening of their own accord.
Sir, this stranger who has come to Thebes is full
of many miracles. I know no more than that.
The rest is your affair.

Pentheus

Untie his hands.
We have him in our net. He may be quick,
but he cannot escape us now, I think.

(*While the servants untie Dionysus' hands, Pentheus attentively scrutinizes his prisoner. Then the servants step back, leaving Pentheus and Dionysus face to face.*)

So,
you *are* attractive, stranger, at least to women—
which explains, I think, your presence here in Thebes.
Your curls are long. You do not wrestle, I take it.
And what fair skin you have—you must take care of it—
no daylight complexion; no, it comes from the night
when you hunt Aphrodite with your beauty.
Now then,
who are you and from where?

Dionysus

It is nothing
to boast of and easily told. You have heard, I suppose,
of Mount Tmolus and her flowers?

Pentheus

I know the place.
It rings the city of Sardis.

Dionysus

I come from there.
My country is Lydia.

Pentheus

Who is this god whose worship
you have imported into Hellas?

Dionysus

Dionysus, the son of Zeus.
He initiated me.

Pentheus

You have some local Zeus
who spawns new gods?

Dionysus

He is the same as yours—
the Zeus who married Semele.

Pentheus

How did you see him?
In a dream or face to face?

Dionysus

Face to face.
He gave me his rites.

Pentheus

What form do they take,
these mysteries of yours?

Dionysus

It is forbidden
to tell the uninitiate.

Pentheus

Tell me the benefits
that those who know your mysteries enjoy.

Dionysus

I am forbidden to say. But they are worth knowing.

Pentheus

Your answers are designed to make me curious.

Dionysus

No:
our mysteries abhor an unbelieving man.

Pentheus

You say you saw the god. What form did he assume?

Dionysus

Whatever form he wished. The choice was his,
not mine.

Pentheus

You evade the question.

Dionysus

Talk sense to a fool
and he calls you foolish.

Pentheus

Have you introduced your rites
in other cities too? Or is Thebes the first?

Dionysus

Foreigners everywhere now dance for Dionysus.

Pentheus

They are more ignorant than Greeks.

Dionysus

In this matter
they are not. Customs differ.

Pentheus

Do you hold your rites
during the day or night?

Dionysus

Mostly by night.
The darkness is well suited to devotion.

Pentheus

Better suited to lechery and seducing women.

Dionysus

You can find debauchery by daylight too.

Pentheus

You shall regret these clever answers.

Dionysus

And you,
your stupid blasphemies.

Pentheus

What a bold bacchant!
You wrestle well—when it comes to words.

Dionysus

Tell me,
what punishment do you propose?

Pentheus

First of all,
I shall cut off your girlish curls.

Dionysus

My hair is holy.
My curls belong to god.

(*Pentheus shears away the god's curls.*)

Pentheus

Second, you will surrender
your wand.

Dionysus

You take it. It belongs to Dionysus.

(*Pentheus takes the thyrsus.*)

Pentheus

Last, I shall place you under guard and confine you
in the palace.

Dionysus

The god himself will set me free
whenever I wish.

Pentheus

You will be with your women in prison
when you call on him for help.

Dionysus

He is here now
and sees what I endure from you.

Pentheus

Where is he?
I cannot see him.

Dionysus

With me. Your blasphemies
have made you blind.

Pentheus (*to attendants*)

Seize him. He is mocking me
and Thebes.

Dionysus

I give you sober warning, fools:
place no chains on *me*.

Pentheus

But *I* say: chain him.
And I am the stronger here.

Dionysus

You do not know
the limits of your strength. You do not know
what you do. You do not know who you are.

Pentheus

I am Pentheus, the son of Echion and Agave.

Dionysus

Pentheus: you shall repent that name.

Pentheus

Off with him.
Chain his hands; lock him in the stables by the palace.
Since he desires the darkness, give him what he wants.
Let him dance down there in the dark.

(*As the attendants bind Dionysus' hands, the Chorus beats on its drums with increasing agitation as though to emphasize the sacrilege.*)

As for these women,
your accomplices in making trouble here,
I shall have them sold as slaves or put to work
at my looms. That will silence their drums.

(*Exit Pentheus.*)

Dionysus

I go,
though not to suffer, since that cannot be.
But Dionysus whom you outrage by your acts,

who you deny is god, will call you to account.
When you set chains on me, you manacle the god.

(*Exeunt attendants with Dionysus captive.*)

Chorus

—O Dirce, holy river,
child of Achelöus' water,
yours the springs that welcomed once
divinity, the son of Zeus!
For Zeus the father snatched his son
from deathless flame, crying:
Dithyrambus, come!
Enter my male womb.
I name you Bacchus and to Thebes
proclaim you by that name.
But now, O blessèd Dirce,
you banish me when to your banks I come,
crowned with ivy, bringing revels.
O Dirce, why am I rejected?
By the clustered grapes I swear,
by Dionysus' wine,
someday you shall come to know
the name of *Bromius!*

—With fury, with fury, he rages,
Pentheus, son of Echion,
born of the breed of Earth,
spawned by the dragon, whelped by Earth!
Inhuman, a rabid beast,
a giant in wildness raging,
storming, defying the children of heaven.
He has threatened me with bonds
though my body is bound to god.
He cages my comrades with chains;
he has cast them in prison darkness.
O lord, son of Zeus, do you see?

O Dionysus, do you see
how in shackles we are held
unbreakably, in the bonds of oppressors?
Descend from Olympus, lord!
Come, whirl your wand of gold
and quell with death this beast of blood
whose violence abuses man and god
outrageously.

—O lord, where do you wave your wand
among the running companies of god?
There on Nysa, mother of beasts?
There on the ridges of Corycia?
Or there among the forests of Olympus
where Orpheus fingered his lyre
and mustered with music the trees,
mustered the wilderness beasts?
O Pieria, you are blessed!
Evius honors you. He comes to dance,
bringing his Bacchae, fording the race
where Axios runs, bringing his Maenads
whirling over Lydias,
generous father of rivers
and famed for his lovely waters
that fatten a land of good horses.

(*Thunder and lightning. The earth trembles. The Chorus is crazed with fear.*)

Dionysus (*from within*)

Ho!
Hear me! Ho, Bacchae!
Ho, Bacchae! Hear my cry!

Chorus

Who cries?
Who calls me with that cry
of Evius? Where are you, lord?

Dionysus

Ho! Again I cry—
the son of Zeus and Semele!

Chorus

O lord, lord Bromius!
Bromius, come to us now!

Dionysus

Let the earthquake come! Shatter the floor of the world!

Chorus

—Look there, how the palace of Pentheus totters.
—Look, the palace is collapsing!
—Dionysus is within. Adore him!
—We adore him!
—Look there!
—Above the pillars, how the great stones
gape and crack!
—Listen. Bromius cries his victory!

Dionysus

Launch the blazing thunderbolt of god! O lightnings,
come! Consume with flame the palace of Pentheus!

(*A burst of lightning flares across the façade of the palace and tongues of flame spurt up from the tomb of Semele. Then a great crash of thunder.*)

Chorus

Ah,
look how the fire leaps up
on the holy tomb of Semele,
the flame of Zeus of Thunders,
his lightnings, still alive,
blazing where they fell!
Down, Maenads,
fall to the ground in awe! He walks
among the ruins he has made!

He has brought the high house low!
He comes, our god, the son of Zeus!

(The Chorus falls to the ground in oriental fashion, bowing their heads in the direction of the palace. A hush; then Dionysus appears, lightly picking his way among the rubble. Calm and smiling still, he speaks to the Chorus with a solicitude approaching banter.)

Dionysus

What, women of Asia? Were you so overcome with fright
you fell to the ground? I think then you must have seen
how Bacchus jostled the palace of Pentheus. But come, rise.
Do not be afraid.

Coryphaeus

O greatest light of our holy revels,
how glad I am to see your face! Without you I was lost.

Dionysus

Did you despair when they led me away to cast me down
in the darkness of Pentheus' prison?

Coryphaeus

What else could I do?
Where would I turn for help if something happened to you?
But how did you escape that godless man?

Dionysus

With ease.
No effort was required.

Coryphaeus

But the manacles on your wrists?

Dionysus

There I, in turn, humiliated him, outrage for outrage.
He seemed to think that he was chaining me but never once

so much as touched my hands. He fed on his desires.
Inside the stable he intended as my jail, instead of me,
he found a bull and tried to rope its knees and hooves.
He was panting desperately, biting his lips with his teeth,
his whole body drenched with sweat, while I sat nearby,
quietly watching. But at that moment Bacchus came,
shook the palace and touched his mother's grave with tongues
of fire. Imagining the palace was in flames,
Pentheus went rushing here and there, shouting to his slaves
to bring him water. Every hand was put to work: in vain.
Then, afraid I might escape, he suddenly stopped short,
drew his sword and rushed to the palace. There, it seems,
Bromius had made a shape, a phantom which resembled me,
within the court. Bursting in, Pentheus thrust and stabbed
at that thing of gleaming air as though he thought it me.
And then, once again, the god humiliated him.
He razed the palace to the ground where it lies, shattered
in utter ruin—his reward for my imprisonment.
At that bitter sight, Pentheus dropped his sword, exhausted
by the struggle. A man, a man, and nothing more,
yet he presumed to wage a war with god.
For my part,
I left the palace quietly and made my way outside.
For Pentheus I care nothing.
But judging from the sound
of tramping feet inside the court, I think our man
will soon be here. What, I wonder, will he have to say?
But let him bluster. I shall not be touched to rage.
Wise men know constraint: our passions are controlled.

(*Enter Pentheus, stamping heavily, from the ruined palace.*)

Pentheus

But this is mortifying. That stranger, that man
I clapped in irons, has escaped.

(*He catches sight of Dionysus.*)

What! *You?*
Well, what do you have to say for yourself?
How did you escape? Answer me.

Dionysus

Your anger
walks too heavily. Tread lightly here.

Pentheus

How did you escape?

Dionysus

Don't you remember?
Someone, I said, would set me free.

Pentheus

Someone?
But who? Who is this mysterious someone?

Dionysus

[He who makes the grape grow its clusters
for mankind.]

Pentheus

A splendid contribution, that.

Dionysus

You disparage the gift that is his chiefest glory.

Pentheus

[If I catch him here, he will not escape my anger.]
I shall order every gate in every tower
to be bolted tight.

Dionysus

And so? Could not a god
hurdle your city walls?

Pentheus

You are clever—very—
but not where it counts.

Dionysus

Where it counts the most,
there I *am* clever.

(*Enter a messenger, a herdsman from Mount Cithaeron.*)

But hear this messenger
who brings you news from the mountain of Cithaeron.
We shall remain where we are. Do not fear:
we will not run away.

Messenger

Pentheus, king of Thebes,
I come from Cithaeron where the gleaming flakes of snow
fall on and on forever—

Pentheus

Get to the point.
What is your message, man?

Messenger

Sir, I have seen
the holy Maenads, the women who ran barefoot
and crazy from the city, and I wanted to report
to you and Thebes what weird fantastic things,
what miracles and more than miracles,
these women do. But may I speak freely
in my own way and words, or make it short?
I fear the harsh impatience of your nature, sire,
too kingly and too quick to anger.

Pentheus

Speak freely.
You have my promise: I shall not punish you.
Displeasure with a man who speaks the truth is wrong.
However, the more terrible this tale of yours,
that much more terrible will be the punishment
I impose upon that man who taught our womenfolk
this strange new magic.

Messenger

About that hour
when the sun lets loose its light to warm the earth,
our grazing herds of cows had just begun to climb
the path along the mountain ridge. Suddenly
I saw three companies of dancing women,
one led by Autonoë, the second captained
by your mother Agave, while Ino led the third.
There they lay in the deep sleep of exhaustion,
some resting on boughs of fir, others sleeping
where they fell, here and there among the oak leaves—
but all modestly and soberly, not, as you think,
drunk with wine, nor wandering, led astray
by the music of the flute, to hunt their Aphrodite
through the woods.

But your mother heard the lowing
of our hornèd herds, and springing to her feet,
gave a great cry to waken them from sleep.
And they too, rubbing the bloom of soft sleep
from their eyes, rose up lightly and straight—
a lovely sight to see: all as one,
the old women and the young and the unmarried girls.
First they let their hair fall loose, down
over their shoulders, and those whose straps had slipped
fastened their skins of fawn with writhing snakes
that licked their cheeks. Breasts swollen with milk,
new mothers who had left their babies behind at home
nestled gazelles and young wolves in their arms,
suckling them. Then they crowned their hair with leaves,
ivy and oak and flowering bryony. One woman
struck her thyrsus against a rock and a fountain
of cool water came bubbling up. Another drove
her fennel in the ground, and where it struck the earth,
at the touch of god, a spring of wine poured out.
Those who wanted milk scratched at the soil
with bare fingers and the white milk came welling up.

Pure honey spurted, streaming, from their wands.
If you had been there and seen these wonders for yourself,
you would have gone down on your knees and prayed
to the god you now deny.
We cowherds and shepherds
gathered in small groups, wondering and arguing
among ourselves at these fantastic things,
the awful miracles those women did.
But then a city fellow with the knack of words
rose to his feet and said: "All you who live
upon the pastures of the mountain, what do you say?
Shall we earn a little favor with King Pentheus
by hunting his mother Agave out of the revels?"
Falling in with his suggestion, we withdrew
and set ourselves in ambush, hidden by the leaves
among the undergrowth. Then at a signal
all the Bacchae whirled their wands for the revels
to begin. With one voice they cried aloud:
"*O Iacchus! Son of Zeus!*" "*O Bromius!*" they cried
until the beasts and all the mountain seemed
wild with divinity. And when they ran,
everything ran with them.
It happened, however,
that Agave ran near the ambush where I lay
concealed. Leaping up, I tried to seize her,
but she gave a cry: "Hounds who run with me,
men are hunting us down! Follow, follow me!
Use your wands for weapons."
At this we fled
and barely missed being torn to pieces by the women.
Unarmed, they swooped down upon the herds of cattle
grazing there on the green of the meadow. And then
you could have seen a single woman with bare hands
tear a fat calf, still bellowing with fright,
in two, while others clawed the heifers to pieces.
There were ribs and cloven hooves scattered everywhere,

and scraps smeared with blood hung from the fir trees.
And bulls, their raging fury gathered in their horns,
lowered their heads to charge, then fell, stumbling
to the earth, pulled down by hordes of women
and stripped of flesh and skin more quickly, sire,
than you could blink your royal eyes. Then,
carried up by their own speed, they flew like birds
across the spreading fields along Asopus' stream
where most of all the ground is good for harvesting.
Like invaders they swooped on Hysiae
and on Erythrae in the foothills of Cithaeron.
Everything in sight they pillaged and destroyed.
They snatched the children from their homes. And when
they piled their plunder on their backs, it stayed in place,
untied. Nothing, neither bronze nor iron,
fell to the dark earth. Flames flickered
in their curls and did not burn them. Then the villagers,
furious at what the women did, took to arms.
And *there*, sire, was something terrible to see.
For the men's spears were pointed and sharp, and yet
drew no blood, whereas the wands the women threw
inflicted wounds. And then the men *ran*,
routed by women! Some god, I say, was with them.
The Bacchae then returned where they had started,
by the springs the god had made, and washed their hands
while the snakes licked away the drops of blood
that dabbled their cheeks.

Whoever this god may be,
sire, welcome him to Thebes. For he is great
in many other ways as well. It was he,
or so they say, who gave to mortal men
the gift of lovely wine by which our suffering
is stopped. And if there is no god of wine,
there is no love, no Aphrodite either,
nor other pleasure left to men.

(*Exit messenger.*)

Coryphaeus

I tremble
to speak the words of freedom before the tyrant.
But let the truth be told: there is no god
greater than Dionysus.

Pentheus

Like a blazing fire
this Bacchic violence spreads. It comes too close.
We are disgraced, humiliated in the eyes
of Hellas. This is no time for hesitation.

(*He turns to an attendant.*)

You there. Go down quickly to the Electran gates
and order out all heavy-armored infantry;
call up the fastest troops among our cavalry,
the mobile squadrons and the archers. We march
against the Bacchae! Affairs are out of hand
when we tamely endure such conduct in our women.

(*Exit attendant.*)

Dionysus

Pentheus, you do not hear, or else you disregard
my words of warning. You have done me wrong,
and yet, in spite of that, I warn you once
again: do not take arms against a god.
Stay quiet here. Bromius will not let you
drive his women from their revels on the mountain.

Pentheus

Don't you lecture me. You escaped from prison.
Or shall I punish you again?

Dionysus

If I were you,
I would offer him a sacrifice, not rage
and kick against necessity, a man defying
god.

Pentheus

I shall give your god the sacrifice
that he deserves. His victims will be his women.
I shall make a great slaughter in the woods of Cithaeron.

Dionysus

You will all be routed, shamefully defeated,
when their wands of ivy turn back your shields
of bronze.

Pentheus

It is hopeless to wrestle with this man.
Nothing on earth will make him hold his tongue.

Dionysus

Friend,
you can still save the situation.

Pentheus

How?
By accepting orders from my own slaves?

Dionysus

No.
I undertake to lead the women back to Thebes.
Without bloodshed.

Pentheus

This is some trap.

Dionysus

A trap?
How so, if I save you by my own devices?

Pentheus

I know.
You and they have conspired to establish your rites
forever.

Dionysus

True, I *have* conspired—with god.

Pentheus

Bring my armor, someone. And *you* stop talking.

(*Pentheus strides toward the left, but when he is almost offstage, Dionysus calls imperiously to him.*)

Dionysus

Wait!
Would you like to *see* their revels on the mountain?

Pentheus

I would pay a great sum to see that sight.

Dionysus

Why are you so passionately curious?

Pentheus

Of course
I'd be sorry to see them drunk—

Dionysus

But for all your sorrow,
you'd like very much to see them?

Pentheus

Yes, very much.
I could crouch beneath the fir trees, out of sight.

Dionysus

But if you try to hide, they may track you down.

Pentheus

Your point is well taken. I will go openly.

Dionysus

Shall I lead you there now? Are you ready to go?

Pentheus

The sooner the better. The loss of even a moment
would be disappointing now.

Dionysus

First, however,
you must dress yourself in women's clothes.

Pentheus

What?
You want *me*, a man, to wear a woman's dress. But why?

Dionysus

If they knew you were a man, they would kill you instantl

Pentheus

True. You are an old hand at cunning, I see.

Dionysus

Dionysus taught me everything I know.

Pentheus

Your advice is to the point. What I fail to see
is what we do.

Dionysus

I shall go inside with you
and help you dress.

Pentheus

Dress? In a *woman's* dress,
you mean? I would die of shame.

Dionysus

Very well.
Then you no longer hanker to see the Maenads?

Pentheus

What is this costume I must wear?

Dionysus

On your head
I shall set a wig with long curls.

Pentheus

And then?

Dionysus

Next, robes to your feet and a net for your hair.

Pentheus

Yes? Go on.

Dionysus

Then a thyrsus for your hand
and a skin of dappled fawn.

Pentheus

I could not bear it.
I *cannot* bring myself to dress in women's clothes.

Dionysus

Then you must fight the Bacchae. That means bloodshed.

Pentheus

Right. First we must go and reconnoiter.

Dionysus

Surely a wiser course than that of hunting bad
with worse.

Pentheus

But how can we pass through the city
without being seen?

Dionysus

We shall take deserted streets.
I will lead the way.

Pentheus

Any way you like,
provided those women of Bacchus don't jeer at me.
First, however, I shall ponder your advice,
whether to go or not.

Dionysus

Do as you please.
I am ready, whatever you decide.

Pentheus

Yes.
Either I shall march with my army to the mountain
or act on your advice.

(*Exit Pentheus into the palace.*)

Dionysus

Women, our prey now thrashes
in the net we threw. He shall see the Bacchae
and pay the price with death.
O Dionysus,
now action rests with you. And you are near.
Punish this man. But first distract his wits;
bewilder him with madness. For sane of mind
this man would never wear a woman's dress;
but obsess his soul and he will not refuse.
After those threats with which he was so fierce,
I want him made the laughingstock of Thebes,
paraded through the streets, a woman.
Now
I shall go and costume Pentheus in the clothes
which he must wear to Hades when he dies, butchered
by the hands of his mother. He shall come to know
Dionysus, son of Zeus, consummate god,
most terrible, and yet most gentle, to mankind.

(*Exit Dionysus into the palace.*)

Chorus

—When shall I dance once more
with bare feet the all-night dances,
tossing my head for joy
in the damp air, in the dew,
as a running fawn might frisk
for the green joy of the wide fields,

free from fear of the hunt,
free from the circling beaters
and the nets of woven mesh
and the hunters hallooing on
their yelping packs? And then, hard pressed,
she sprints with the quickness of wind,
bounding over the marsh, leaping
to frisk, leaping for joy,
gay with the green of the leaves,
to dance for joy in the forest,
to dance where the darkness is deepest,
where no man is.

—What is wisdom? What gift of the gods
is held in honor like this:
to hold your hand victorious
over the heads of those you hate?
Honor is precious forever.

—Slow but unmistakable
the might of the gods moves on.
It punishes that man,
infatuate of soul
and hardened in his pride,
who disregards the gods.
The gods are crafty:
they lie in ambush
a long step of time
to hunt the unholy.
Beyond the old beliefs,
no thought, no act shall go.
Small, small is the cost
to believe in this:
whatever is god is strong;
whatever long time has sanctioned,
that is a law forever;
the law tradition makes
is the law of nature.

—What is wisdom? What gift of the gods
is held in honor like this:
to hold your hand victorious
over the heads of those you hate?
Honor is precious forever.

—Blessèd is he who escapes a storm at sea,
who comes home to his harbor.
—Blessèd is he who emerges from under affliction.
—In various ways one man outraces another in the
race for wealth and power.
—Ten thousand men possess ten thousand hopes.
—A few bear fruit in happiness; the others go awry.
—But he who garners day by day the good of life,
he is happiest. Blessèd is he.

(Re-enter Dionysus from the palace. At the threshold he turns and calls back to Pentheus.)

Dionysus

Pentheus if you are still so curious to see
forbidden sights, so bent on evil still,
come out. Let us see you in your woman's dress,
disguised in Maenad clothes so you may go and spy
upon your mother and her company.

(Enter Pentheus from the palace. He wears a long linen dress which partially conceals his fawn-skin. He carries a thyrsus in his hand; on his head he wears a wig with long blond curls bound by a snood. He is dazed and completely in the power of the god who has now possessed him.)

Why,
you look exactly like one of the daughters of Cadmus.

Pentheus

I seem to see two suns blazing in the heavens.
And now two Thebes, two cities, and each
with seven gates. And you—you are a bull

who walks before me there. Horns have sprouted
from your head. Have you always been a beast?
But now I see a bull.

Dionysus

It is the god you see.
Though hostile formerly, he now declares a truce
and goes with us. You see what you could not
when you were blind.

Pentheus (coyly primping)

Do I look like anyone?
Like Ino or my mother Agave?

Dionysus

So much alike
I almost might be seeing one of them. But look:
one of your curls has come loose from under the snood
where I tucked it.

Pentheus

It must have worked loose
when I was dancing for joy and shaking my head.

Dionysus

Then let me be your maid and tuck it back.
Hold still.

Pentheus

Arrange it. I am in your hands
completely.

(Dionysus tucks the curl back under the snood.)

Dionysus

And now your strap has slipped. Yes,
and your robe hangs askew at the ankles.

Pentheus (bending backward to look)

I think so.
At least on my right leg. But on the left the hem
lies straight.

Dionysus

You will think me the best of friends
when you see to your surprise how chaste the Bacchae are.

Pentheus

But to be a real Bacchante, should I hold
the wand in my right hand? Or this way?

Dionysus

No.
In your right hand. And raise it as you raise
your right foot. I commend your change of heart.

Pentheus

Could I lift Cithaeron up, do you think?
Shoulder the cliffs, Bacchae and all?

Dionysus

If you wanted.
Your mind was once unsound, but now you think
as sane men do.

Pentheus

Should we take crowbars with us?
Or should I put my shoulder to the cliffs
and heave them up?

Dionysus

What? And destroy the haunts
of the nymphs, the holy groves where Pan plays
his woodland pipe?

Pentheus

You are right. In any case,
women should not be mastered by brute strength.
I will hide myself beneath the firs instead.

Dionysus

You will find all the ambush you deserve,
creeping up to spy on the Maenads.

Pentheus

Think.

I can see them already, there among the bushes,
mating like birds, caught in the toils of love.

Dionysus

Exactly. This is your mission: you go to watch.
You may surprise them—or they may surprise you.

Pentheus

Then lead me through the very heart of Thebes,
since I, alone of all this city, dare to go.

Dionysus

You and you alone will suffer for your city.
A great ordeal awaits you. But you are worthy
of your fate. I shall lead you safely there;
someone else shall bring you back.

Pentheus

Yes, my mother.

Dionysus

An example to all men.

Pentheus

It is for that I go.

Dionysus

You will be carried home—

Pentheus

O luxury!

Dionysus

cradled in your mother's arms.

Pentheus

You will spoil me.

Dionysus

I *mean* to spoil you.

Pentheus

I go to my reward.

Dionysus

You are an extraordinary young man, and you go
to an extraordinary experience. You shall win
a glory towering to heaven and usurping
god's.

(*Exit Pentheus.*)

Agave and you daughters of Cadmus,
reach out your hands! I bring this young man
to a great ordeal. The victor? Bromius.
Bromius—and I. The rest the event shall show.

(*Exit Dionysus.*)

Chorus

—Run to the mountain, fleet hounds of madness!
Run, run to the revels of Cadmus' daughters!
Sting them against the man in women's clothes,
the madman who spies on the Maenads, who peers
from behind the rocks, who spies from a vantage!
His mother shall see him first. She will cry
to the Maenads: "Who is this spy who has come
to the mountains to peer at the mountain-revels
of the women of Thebes? What bore him, Bacchae?
This man was born of no woman. Some lioness
give him birth, some one of the Libyan gorgons!"

—O Justice, principle of order, spirit of custom,
come! Be manifest; reveal yourself with a sword!
Stab through the throat that godless man,
the mocker who goes, flouting custom and outraging god!
O Justice, stab the evil earth-born spawn of Echion!

—Uncontrollable, the unbeliever goes,
in spitting rage, rebellious and amok,
madly assaulting the mysteries of god,
profaning the rites of the mother of god.

Against the unassailable he runs, with rage
obsessed. Headlong he runs to death.
For death the gods exact, curbing by that bit
the mouths of men. They humble us with death
that we remember what we are who are not god,
but men. We run to death. Wherefore, I say,
accept, accept:
humility is wise; humility is blest.
But what the world calls wise I do not want.
Elsewhere the chase. I hunt another game,
those great, those manifest, those certain goals,
achieving which, our mortal lives are blest.
Let these things be the quarry of my chase:
purity; humility; an unrebellious soul,
accepting all. Let me go the customary way,
the timeless, honored, beaten path of those who walk
with reverence and awe beneath the sons of heaven.

—O Justice, principle of order, spirit of custom,
come! Be manifest; reveal yourself with a sword!
Stab through the throat that godless man,
the mocker who goes, flouting custom and outraging god!
O Justice, destroy the evil earth-born sprawn of Echion!

—O Dionysus, reveal yourself a bull! Be manifest,
a snake with darting heads, a lion breathing fire!
O Bacchus, come! Come with your smile!
Cast your noose about this man who hunts
your Bacchae! Bring him down, trampled
underfoot by the murderous herd of your Maenads!

(*Enter a messenger from Cithaeron.*)

Messenger

How prosperous in Hellas these halls once were,
this house founded by Cadmus, the stranger from Sidon
who sowed the dragon seed in the land of the snake!

I am a slave and nothing more, yet even so
I mourn the fortunes of this fallen house.

Coryphaeus

What is it?
Is there news of the Bacchae?

Messenger

This is my news:
Pentheus, the son of Echion, is dead.

Coryphaeus

All hail to Bromius! Our god is a great god!

Messenger

What is this you say, women? You dare to rejoice
at these disasters which destroy this house?

Coryphaeus

I am no Greek. I hail my god
in my own way. No longer need I
shrink with fear of prison.

Messenger

If you suppose this city is so short of men—

Coryphaeus

Dionysus, Dionysus, not Thebes,
has power over me.

Messenger

Your feelings might be forgiven, then. But this,
this exultation in disaster—it is not right.

Coryphaeus

Tell us how the mocker died.
How was he killed?

Messenger

There were three of us in all: Pentheus and I,
attending my master, and that stranger who volunteered
his services as guide. Leaving behind us
the last outlying farms of Thebes, we forded
the Asopus and struck into the barren scrubland
of Cithaeron.
There in a grassy glen we halted,
unmoving, silent, without a word,
so we might see but not be seen. From that vantage,
in a hollow cut from the sheer rock of the cliffs,
a place where water ran and the pines grew dense
with shade, we saw the Maenads sitting, their hands
busily moving at their happy tasks. Some
wound the stalks of their tattered wands with tendrils
of fresh ivy; others, frisking like fillies
newly freed from the painted bridles, chanted
in Bacchic songs, responsively.
But Pentheus—
unhappy man—could not quite see the companies
of women. "Stranger," he said, "from where I stand,
I cannot see these counterfeited Maenads.
But if I climbed that towering fir that overhangs
the banks, then I could see their shameless orgies
better."
And now the stranger worked a miracle.
Reaching for the highest branch of a great fir,
he bent it down, down, down to the dark earth,
till it was curved the way a taut bow bends
or like a rim of wood when forced about the circle
of a wheel. Like that he forced that mountain fir
down to the ground. No mortal could have done it.
Then he seated Pentheus at the highest tip
and with his hands let the trunk rise straightly up,
slowly and gently, lest it throw its rider.
And the tree rose, towering to heaven, with my master

huddled at the top. And now the Maenads saw him
more clearly than he saw them. But barely had they seen,
when the stranger vanished and there came a great voice
out of heaven—Dionysus', it must have been—
crying: "Women, I bring you the man who has mocked
at you and me and at our holy mysteries.
Take vengeance upon him." And as he spoke
a flash of awful fire bound earth and heaven.
The high air hushed, and along the forest glen
the leaves hung still; you could hear no cry of beasts.
The Bacchae heard that voice but missed its words,
and leaping up, they stared, peering everywhere.
Again that voice. And now they knew his cry,
the clear command of god. And breaking loose
like startled doves, through grove and torrent,
over jagged rocks, they flew, their feet maddened
by the breath of god. And when they saw my master
perching in his tree, they climbed a great stone
that towered opposite his perch and showered him
with stones and javelins of fir, while the others
hurled their wands. And yet they missed their target,
poor Pentheus in his perch, barely out of reach
of their eager hands, treed, unable to escape.
Finally they splintered branches from the oaks
and with those bars of wood tried to lever up the tree
by prying at the roots. But every effort failed.
Then Agave cried out: "Maenads, make a circle
about the trunk and grip it with your hands.
Unless we take this climbing beast, he will reveal
the secrets of the god." With that, thousands of hands
tore the fir tree from the earth, and down, down
from his high perch fell Pentheus, tumbling
to the ground, sobbing and screaming as he fell,
for he knew his end was near. His own mother,
like a priestess with her victim, fell upon him
first. But snatching off his wig and snood

so she would recognize his face, he touched her cheeks,
screaming, "*No, no, Mother! I am Pentheus,*
your own son, the child you bore to Echion!
Pity me, spare me, Mother! I have done a wrong,
but do not kill your own son for my offense."
But she was foaming at the mouth, and her crazed eyes
rolling with frenzy. She was mad, stark mad,
possessed by Bacchus. Ignoring his cries of pity,
she seized his left arm at the wrist; then, planting
her foot upon his chest, she pulled, wrenching away
the arm at the shoulder—not by her own strength,
for the god had put inhuman power in her hands.
Ino, meanwhile, on the other side, was scratching off
his flesh. Then Autonoë and the whole horde
of Bacchae swarmed upon him. Shouts everywhere,
he screaming with what little breath was left,
they shrieking in triumph. One tore off an arm,
another a foot still warm in its shoe. His ribs
were clawed clean of flesh and every hand
was smeared with blood as they played ball with scraps
of Pentheus' body.
The pitiful remains lie scattered,
one piece among the sharp rocks, others
lying lost among the leaves in the depths
of the forest. His mother, picking up his head,
impaled it on her wand. She seems to think it is
some mountain lion's head which she carries in triumph
through the thick of Cithaeron. Leaving her sisters
at the Maenad dances, she is coming here, gloating
over her grisly prize. She calls upon Bacchus:
he is her "fellow-huntsman," "comrade of the chase,
crowned with victory." But all the victory
she carries home is her own grief.
Now,
before Agave returns, let me leave
this scene of sorrow. Humility,

a sense of reverence before the sons of heaven—
of all the prizes that a mortal man might win,
these, I say, are wisest; these are best.

(*Exit Messenger.*)

Chorus

—We dance to the glory of Bacchus!
We dance to the death of Pentheus,
the death of the spawn of the dragon!
He dressed in woman's dress;
he took the lovely thyrsus;
it waved him down to death,
led by a bull to Hades.
Hail, Bacchae! Hail, women of Thebes!
Your victory is fair, fair the prize,
this famous prize of grief!
Glorious the game! To fold your child
in your arms, streaming with his blood!

Coryphaeus

But look: there comes Pentheus' mother, Agave,
running wild-eyed toward the palace.
—Welcome,
welcome to the reveling band of the god of joy!

(*Enter Agave with other Bacchantes. She is covered with blood and carries the head of Pentheus impaled upon her thyrsus.*)

Agave

Bacchae of Asia—

Chorus

Speak, speak.

Agave

We bring this branch to the palace,
this fresh-cut spray from the mountains.
Happy was the hunting.

Chorus

I see.
I welcome our fellow-reveler of god.

Agave

The whelp of a wild mountain lion,
and snared by me without a noose.
Look, look at the prize I bring.

Chorus

Where was he caught?

Agave

On Cithaeron—

Chorus

On Cithaeron?

Agave

Our prize was killed.

Chorus

Who killed him?

Agave

I struck him first.
The Maenads call me "Agave the blest."

Chorus

And then?

Agave

Cadmus'—

Chorus

Cadmus'?

Agave

Daughters.
After me, they reached the prey.
After me. Happy was the hunting.

Chorus

Happy indeed.

Agave

Then share my glory,
share the feast.

Chorus

Share, unhappy woman?

Agave

See, the whelp is young and tender.
Beneath the soft mane of its hair,
the down is blooming on the cheeks.

Chorus

With that mane he *looks* a beast.

Agave

Our god is wise. Cunningly, cleverly,
Bacchus the hunter lashed the Maenads
against his prey.

Chorus

Our king is a hunter.

Agave

You praise me now?

Chorus

I praise you.

Agave

The men of Thebes—

Chorus

And Pentheus, your son?

Agave

Will praise his mother. She caught
a great quarry, this lion's cub.

Chorus

Extraordinary catch.

Agave

Extraordinary skill.

Chorus

You are proud?

Agave

Proud and happy.
I have won the trophy of the chase,
a great prize, manifest to all.

Coryphaeus

Then, poor woman, show the citizens of Thebes
this great prize, this trophy you have won
in the hunt.

(*Agave proudly exhibits her thyrsus with the head of Pentheus impaled upon the point.*)

Agave

You citizens of this towered city,
men of Thebes, behold the trophy of your women's
hunting! *This* is the quarry of our chase, taken
not with nets nor spears of bronze but by the white
and delicate hands of women. What are they worth,
your boastings now and all that uselessness
your armor is, since we, with our bare hands,
captured this quarry and tore its bleeding body
limb from limb?
—But where is my father Cadmus?
He should come. And my son. Where is Pentheus?
Fetch him. I will have him set his ladder up
against the wall and, there upon the beam,
nail the head of this wild lion I have killed
as a trophy of my hunt.

(*Enter Cadmus, followed by attendants who bear upon a bier the dismembered body of Pentheus.*)

Cadmus

Follow me, attendants.
Bear your dreadful burden in and set it down,
there before the palace.

(*The attendants set down the bier.*)

This was Pentheus
whose body, after long and weary searchings
I painfully assembled from Cithaeron's glens
where it lay, scattered in shreads, dismembered
throughout the forest, no two pieces
in a single place.
Old Teiresias and I
had returned to Thebes from the orgies on the mountain
before I learned of this atrocious crime
my daughters did. And so I hurried back
to the mountain to recover the body of this boy
murdered by the Maenads. There among the oaks
I found Aristaeus' wife, the mother of Actaeon,
Autonoë, and with her Ino, both
still stung with madness. But Agave, they said,
was on her way to Thebes, still possessed.
And what they said was true, for there she is,
and not a happy sight.

Agave

Now, Father,
yours can be the proudest boast of living men.
For you are now the father of the bravest daughters
in the world. All of your daughters are brave,
but I above the rest. I have left my shuttle
at the loom; I raised my sight to higher things—
to hunting animals with my bare hands.
You see?
Here in my hands I hold the quarry of my chase,
a trophy for our house. Take it, Father, take it.
Glory in my kill and invite your friends to share

the feast of triumph. For you are blest, Father,
by this great deed I have done.

Cadmus

This is a grief
so great it knows no size. I cannot look.
This is the awful murder your hands have done.
This, this is the noble victim you have slaughtered
to the gods. And to share a feast like this
you now invite all Thebes and me?
O gods,
how terribly I pity you and then myself.
Justly—too, too justly—has lord Bromius,
this god of our own blood, destroyed us all,
every one.

Agave

How scowling and crabbed is old age
in men. I hope my son takes after his mother
and wins, as she has done, the laurels of the chase
when he goes hunting with the younger men of Thebes.
But all my son can do is quarrel with god.
He should be scolded, Father, and you are the one
who should scold him. Yes, someone call him out
so he can see his mother's triumph.

Cadmus

Enough. No more.
When you realize the horror you have done,
you shall suffer terribly. But if with luck
your present madness lasts until you die,
you will seem to have, not having, happiness.

Agave

Why do you reproach me? Is there something wrong?

Cadmus

First raise your eyes to the heavens.

Agave

There.
But why?

Cadmus

Does it look the same as it did before?
Or has it changed?

Agave

It seems—somehow—clearer,
brighter than it was before.

Cadmus

Do you still feel
the same flurry inside you?

Agave

The same—flurry?
No, I feel—somehow—calmer. I feel as though—
my mind were somehow—changing.

Cadmus

Can you still hear me?
Can you answer clearly?

Agave

No. I have forgotten
what we were saying, Father.

Cadmus

Who was your husband?

Agave

Echion—a man, they said, born of the dragon seed.

Cadmus

What was the name of the child you bore your husband?

Agave

Pentheus.

Cadmus

And whose head do you hold in your hands?

Agave (averting her eyes)

A lion's head—or so the hunters told me.

Cadmus

Look directly at it. Just a quick glance.

Agave

What is it? What am I holding in my hands?

Cadmus

Look more closely still. Study it carefully.

Agave

No! O gods, I see the greatest grief there is.

Cadmus

Does it look like a lion now?

Agave

No, no. It is—
Pentheus' head—I hold—

Cadmus

And mourned by me
before you ever knew.

Agave

But *who* killed him?
Why am *I* holding him?

Cadmus

O savage truth,
what a time to come!

Agave

For god's sake, speak.
My heart is beating with terror.

Cadmus

You killed him.
You and your sisters.

Agave

But where was he killed?
Here at home? Where?

Cadmus

He was killed on Cithaeron,
there where the hounds tore Actaeon to pieces.

Agave

But why? Why had Pentheus gone to Cithaeron?

Cadmus

He went to your revels to mock the god.

Agave

But *we*—
what were we doing on the mountain?

Cadmus

You were mad.
The whole city was possessed.

Agave

Now, now I see:
Dionysus has destroyed us all.

Cadmus

You outraged him.
You denied that he was truly god.

Agave

Father,
where is my poor boy's body now?

Cadmus

There it is.
I gathered the pieces with great difficulty.

Agave

Is his body entire? Has he been laid out well?

Cadmus

[All but the head. The rest is mutilated
horribly.]

Agave

But why should Pentheus suffer for my crime?

Cadmus

He, like you, blasphemed the god. And so
the god has brought us all to ruin at one blow,
you, your sisters, and this boy. All our house
the god as utterly destroyed and, with it,
me. For I have no sons left, no male heir;
and I have lived only to see this boy,
this branch of your own body, most horribly
and foully killed.

(*He turns and addresses the corpse.*)

—To you my house looked up.
Child, you were the stay of my house; you were
my daughter's son. Of you this city stood in awe.
No one who once had seen your face dared outrage
the old man, or if he did, you punished him.
Now I must go, a banished and dishonored man—
I, Cadmus the great, who sowed the soldiery
of Thebes and harvested a great harvest. My son,
dearest to me of all men—for even dead,
I count you still the man I love the most—
never again will your hand touch my chin;
no more, child, will you hug me and call me
"Grandfather" and say, "Who is wronging you?
Does anyone trouble you or vex your heart, old man?
Tell me, Grandfather, and I will punish him."
No, now there is grief for me; the mourning

for you; pity for your mother; and for her sisters,
sorrow.
If there is still any mortal man
who despises or defies the gods, let him look
on this boy's death and believe in the gods.

Coryphaeus

Cadmus, I pity you. Your daughter's son
has died as he deserved, and yet his death
bears hard on you.

[*At this point there is a break in the manuscript of nearly fifty lines. The following speeches of Agave and Coryphaeus and the first part of Dionysus' speech have been conjecturally reconstructed from fragments and later material which make use of the Bacchae. Lines which can plausibly be assigned to the lacuna are otherwise not indicated. My own inventions are designed, not to complete the speeches, but to effect a transition between the fragments, and are bracketed. For fuller comment, see the Appendix.*—TRANS.]

Agave

O Father, now you can see
how everything has changed. I am in anguish now,
tormented, who walked in triumph minutes past,
exulting in my kill. And that prize I carried home
with such pride was my own curse. Upon these hands
I bear the curse of my son's blood. How then
with these accursed hands may I touch his body?
How can I, accursed with such a curse, hold him
to my breast? O gods, what dirge can I sing
[that there might be] a dirge [for every]
broken limb?

. . . .

Where is a shroud to cover up his corpse?
O my child, what hands will give you proper care
unless with my own hands I lift my curse?

(She lifts up one of Pentheus' limbs and asks the help of Cadmus in piecing the body together. She mourns each piece separately before replacing it on the bier. See Appendix.)

Come, Father. We must restore his head
to this unhappy boy. As best we can, we shall make
him whole again.
—O dearest, dearest face!
Pretty boyish mouth! Now with this veil
I shroud your head, gathering with loving care
these mangled bloody limbs, this flesh I brought
to birth

. . . .

Coryphaeus

Let this scene teach those [who see these things:
Dionysus is the son] of Zeus.

(Above the palace Dionysus appears in epiphany.)

Dionysus

[I am Dionysus,
the son of Zeus, returned to Thebes, revealed,
a god to men.] But the men [of Thebes] blasphemed me.
They slandered me; they said I came of mortal man,
and not content with speaking blasphemies,
[they dared to threaten my person with violence.]
These crimes this people whom I cherished well
did from malice to their benefactor. Therefore,
I now disclose the sufferings in store for them.
Like [enemies], they shall be driven from this city
to other lands; there, submitting to the yoke
of slavery, they shall wear out wretched lives,
captives of war, enduring much indignity.

(He turns to the corpse of Pentheus.)

This man has found the death which he deserved,
torn to pieces among the jagged rocks.
You are my witnesses: he came with outrage;

he attempted to chain my hands, abusing me
[and doing what he should least of all have done.]
And therefore he has rightly perished by the hands
of those who should the least of all have murdered him.
What he suffers, he suffers justly.
Upon you,
Agave, and on your sisters I pronounce this doom:
you shall leave this city in expiation
of the murder you have done. You are unclean,
and it would be a sacrilege that murderers
should remain at peace beside the graves [of those
whom they have killed].

(*He turns to Cadmus.*)

. . . .

Next I shall disclose the trials
which await this man. You, Cadmus, shall be changed
to a serpent, and your wife, the child of Ares,
immortal Harmonia, shall undergo your doom,
a serpent too. With her, it is your fate
to go a journey in a car drawn on by oxen,
leading behind you a great barbarian host.
For thus decrees the oracle of Zeus.
With a host so huge its numbers cannot be counted,
you shall ravage many cities; but when your army
plunders the shrine of Apollo, its homecoming
shall be perilous and hard. Yet in the end
the god Ares shall save Harmonia and you
and bring you both to live among the blest.
So say I, born of no mortal father,
Dionysus, true son of Zeus. If then,
when you would not, you had muzzled your madness,
you should have an ally now in the son of Zeus.

Cadmus

We implore you, Dionysus. We have done wrong.

Dionysus

Too late. When there was time, you did not know me.

Cadmus

We have learned. But your sentence is too harsh.

Dionysus

I am a god. I was blasphemed by you.

Cadmus

Gods should be exempt from human passions.

Dionysus

Long ago my father Zeus ordained these things.

Agave

It is fated, Father. We must go.

Dionysus

Why then delay?
For you must go.

Cadmus

Child, to what a dreadful end
have we all come, you and your wretched sisters
and my unhappy self. An old man, I must go
to live a stranger among barbarian peoples, doomed
to lead against Hellas a motley foreign army.
Transformed to serpents, I and my wife,
Harmonia, the child of Ares, we must captain
spearsmen against the tombs and shrines of Hellas.
Never shall my sufferings end; not even
over Acheron shall I have peace.

Agave (embracing Cadmus)

O Father,
to be banished, to live without you!

Cadmus

Poor child,
like a white swan warding its weak old father,
why do you clasp those white arms about my neck?

Agave

But banished! Where shall I go?

Cadmus

I do not know,
my child. Your father can no longer help you.

Agave

Farewell, my home! City, farewell.
O bridal bed, banished I go,
in misery, I leave you now.

Cadmus

Go, poor child, seek shelter in Aristaeus' house.

Agave

I pity you, Father.

Cadmus

And I pity you, my child,
and I grieve for your poor sisters. I pity them.

Agave

Terribly has Dionysus brought
disaster down upon this house.

Dionysus

I was terribly blasphemed,
my name dishonored in Thebes.

Agave

Farewell, Father.

Cadmus

Farewell to you, unhappy child.
Fare well. But you shall find your faring hard.

(*Exit Cadmus.*)

Agave

Lead me, guides, where my sisters wait,
poor sisters of my exile. Let me go
where I shall never see Cithaeron more,
where that accursed hill may not see me,
where I shall find no trace of thyrsus!
That I leave to other Bacchae.

(*Exit Agave with attendants.*)

Chorus

The gods have many shapes.
The gods bring many things
to their accomplishment.
And what was most expected
has not been accomplished.
But god has found his way
for what no man expected.
So ends the play.

APPENDIX TO *THE BACCHAE*

APPENDIX

Reconstruction of the long lacuna (l. 1329) can never be more than conjectural; but it can at least be that. I have attempted it in the conviction that its presence seriously hinders any possible production of the play.

The contents of the lacuna are, at least in outline, tolerably clear. A third-century rhetorician, Apsines, describes the speech of Agave, how she arouses pity by "picking up in her hands each one of her son's limbs and mourning it individually" (see Apsines *Rhet. Gr.* [ed. Walz], ix. 587). Then, according to the hypothesis of the play, Dionysus appears and addresses all, and foretells the future of each one in turn. The manuscript picks up the speech of Dionysus at line 1330 with an account, virtually complete, of the fate of Cadmus. Against this framework, scholars have been able to place a large number of Euripidean lines from the *Christus Patiens*, a twelfth-century cento, made up of lines from at least seven Euripidean plays. The bulk of the lines which fill the lacuna in my translation come from the *C.P.* Some of them are almost certain; others less so; but together they go a long way toward rounding out the gap. Thorough discussion of the lacuna problem may be found in the commentary on line 1329 in Dodds's edition of *The Bacchae*.

The order of my lines is as follows: beginning, *Bacchae*, l. 1329; *C.P.* ll. 1011, 1311, 1312, 1313, 1256, 1122, 1123; Schol. in Ar. Plut. l. 907; *C.P.* ll. 1466, 1467, 1468, 1469, 1470; Pap. Ant. 24 (*Antinoopolis Pap.* I, ed. C. H. Roberts, 1951) and *C.P.* l. 1472. The speech of Coryphaeus: pap. frag. (cf. Dodds, App. I). The speech of Dionysus: *C.P.* ll. 1360–62, 1665–66, 1668–69, 1678–80, 300; Lucian, *Pisc.* 2; *C.P.* ll. 1692, 1664, 1663, 1667, 1674–78, 1690.

ALCESTIS

Translated by Richmond Lattimore

INTRODUCTION

Alcestis, the earliest extant play of Euripides, was produced in 438 B.C. and won second prize.

The given story was that Admetus, king of Thessaly, could avoid his fated early death if someone else would volunteer to die in his place. Alcestis, his wife, did so; no other would. But Heracles, the friend of Admetus, fought the spirit of Death and took Alcestis away from him and restored her to her husband. The story had been told by Phrynichus, the early-fifth-century tragedian, in a lost satyr-play.

Euripides could have made the main point of his action the heroism of the wife. He does, of course, acknowledge and celebrate this, but the story is really the story of Admetus, the man who let his wife die in his place, his struggle with the unstated fact and final acknowledgment of it. This comes just before her restoration and makes more plausible the miraculous favor shown him by his friends, Apollo and Heracles, as a reward for justice and hospitality. Miracles apart, the play can be read as the study of a good but untried and unready man facing the overwhelming fact of death.

A tragedy with a happy ending, almost a tragedy in reverse, *Alcestis* occupied fourth place in its series and is thus a substitute for the cheerful, ribald satyr-play which customarily concluded the tragic trilogy. It is probably unwise to try to see any elements of satyr-play in it, except for the temporary drunkenness of Heracles, which, as far as it goes, is in the manner of satyr-play and comedy. The choral odes are exceptionally sincere, and throughout the play Euripides' unpretentious style is at its best.

NOTE

The text followed is Murray's Oxford text, and his line numbers, which are standard, have been used, except that different readings have been adopted which affect the translation of the following lines: 50, 124, 223, 943, 1140, 1153.

CHARACTERS

Apollo

Death

Chorus of citizens of Pherae

Maid, attendant of Alcestis

Alcestis, wife of Admetus

Admetus of Pherae, king of Thessaly

Boy (Eumelus), son of Admetus and Alcestis

Heracles

Pheres, father of Admetus

Servant of Admetus

Girl, daughter of Admetus and Alcestis (silent character)

Servants (silent)

ALCESTIS

SCENE: *Pherae, in Thessaly, before the house of Admetus. The front door of the house, or palace, is the center of the backdrop.*

(*Enter Apollo from the house, armed with a bow.*)

Apollo

House of Admetus, in which I, god though I am,
had patience to accept the table of the serfs!
Zeus was the cause. Zeus killed my son, Asclepius,
and drove the bolt of the hot lightning through his chest.
I, in my anger for this, killed the Cyclopes,
smiths of Zeus's fire, for which my father made me serve
a mortal man, in penance for my misdoings.
I came to this country, tended the oxen of this host
and friend, Admetus, son of Pheres. I have kept
his house from danger, cheated the Fates to save his life
until this day, for he revered my sacred rights
sacredly, and the fatal goddesses allowed
Admetus to escape the moment of his death
by giving the lower powers someone else to die
instead of him. He tried his loved ones all in turn,
father and aged mother who had given him birth,
and found not one, except his wife, who would consent
to die for him, and not see daylight any more.
She is in the house now, gathered in his arms and held
at the breaking point of life, because the destiny marks
this for her day of death and taking leave of life.
The stain of death in the house must not be on me. I
step therefore from these chambers dearest to my love.
And here is Death himself, I see him coming, Death
who dedicates the dying, who will lead her down
to the house of Hades. He has come on time. He has
been watching for this day on which her death falls due.

(*Enter Death, armed with a sword, from the wing. He sees Apollo suddenly and shows surprise.*)

Death

Ah!
You at this house, Phoebus? Why do you haunt
the place. It is unfair to take for your own
and spoil the death-spirits' privileges.
Was it not enough, then, that you blocked the death
of Admetus, and overthrew the Fates
by a shabby wrestler's trick? And now
your bow hand is armed to guard her too,
Alcestis, Pelias' daughter, though she
promised her life for her husband's.

Apollo

Never fear. I have nothing but justice and fair words for you.

Death

If you mean fairly, what are you doing with a bow?

Apollo

It is my custom to carry it with me all the time.

Death

It is your custom to help this house more than you ought.

Apollo

But he is my friend, and his misfortunes trouble me.

Death

You mean to take her body, too, away from me?

Apollo

I never took *his* body away from you by force.

Death

How is it, then, that he is above ground, not below?

Apollo

He gave his wife instead, and you have come for her now.

Death

I have. And I shall take her down where the dead are.

Apollo

Take her and go. I am not sure you will listen to me.

Death

Tell me to kill whom I must kill. Such are my orders.

Apollo

No, only to put their death off. They must die in the end.

Death

I understand what you would say and what you want.

Apollo

Is there any way, then, for Alcestis to grow old?

Death

There is not. I insist on enjoying my rights too.

Apollo

You would not take more than one life, in any case.

Death

My privilege means more to me when they die young.

Apollo

If she dies old, she will have a lavish burial.

Death

What you propose, Phoebus, is to favor the rich.

Apollo

What is this? Have you unrecognized talents for debate?

Death

Those who could afford to buy a late death would buy it then.

Apollo

I see. Are you determined not to do this for me?

Death

I will not do it. And you know my character.

Apollo

I know it: hateful to mankind, loathed by the gods.

Death

You cannot always have your way where you should not.

Apollo

For all your brute ferocity you shall be stopped.
The man to do it is on the way to Pheres' house
now, on an errand from Eurystheus, sent to steal
a team of horses from the wintry lands of Thrace.
He shall be entertained here in Admetus' house
and he shall take the woman away from you by force,
nor will you have our gratitude, but you shall still
be forced to do it, and to have my hate beside.

Death

Much talk. Talking will win you nothing. All the same,
the woman goes with me to Hades' house. I go
to take her now, and dedicate her with my sword,
for all whose hair is cut in consecration
by this blade's edge are devoted to the gods below.

(*Death enters the house. Apollo leaves by the wing. The Chorus enters and forms a group before the gates.*)

Chorus

It is quiet by the palace. What does it mean?
Why is the house of Admetus so still?
Is there none here of his family, none
who can tell us whether the queen is dead
and therefore to be mourned? Or does Pelias'
daughter Alcestis live still, still look
on daylight, she who in my mind appears
noble beyond
all women beside in a wife's duty?

(*Here they speak individually, not as a group.*)

First Citizen

Does someone hear anything?

The sound a hand's stroke would make,
or outcry, as if something were done
and over?

Second Citizen

No. And there is no servant stationed
at the outer gates. O Paean,
healer, might you show in light
to still the storm of disaster.

Third Citizen

They would not be silent if she were dead.

Fourth Citizen

No, she is gone.

Fifth Citizen

They have not taken her yet from the house.

Sixth Citizen

So sure? I know nothing. Why are you certain?
And how could Admetus have buried his wife
with none by, and she so splendid?

Seventh Citizen

Here at the gates I do not see
the lustral spring water, approved
by custom for a house of death.

Eighth Citizen

Nor are there cut locks of hair at the forecourts
hanging, such as the stroke of sorrow
for the dead makes. I can hear no beating
of the hands of young women.

Ninth Citizen

Yet this is the day appointed.

Tenth Citizen

What do you mean? Speak.

Ninth Citizen

On which she must pass to the world below.

Eleventh Citizen

You touch me deep, my heart, where it hurts.

Twelfth Citizen

Yes. He who from the first has claimed to be called
a good man himself
must grieve when good men are afflicted.

(*Henceforward all the Chorus together.*)

Sailing the long sea, there is
not any place on earth
you could win, not Lycia,
not the unwatered sands called
of Ammon, not
thus to approach and redeem the life
of this unhappy woman. Her fate shows
steep and near. There is no god's hearth
I know you could reach and by sacrifice
avail to save.

There was only one. If the eyes
of Phoebus' son were opened
still, if he could have come
and left the dark chambers,
the gates of Hades.
He upraised those who were stricken
down, until from the hand of God
the flown bolt of thunder hit him.
Where is there any hope for life
left for me any longer?

For all has been done that can be done by our kings now,
and there on all the gods' altars
are blood sacrifices dripping in full,
but no healing comes for the evil.

(*Enter a maid from the house.*)

Chorus

But here is a serving woman coming from the house.
The tears break from her. What will she say has taken place?
We must, of course, forgive your sorrow if something
has happened to your masters. We should like to know
whether the queen is dead or if she is still alive.

Maid

I could tell you that she is still alive or that she is dead.

Chorus

How could a person both be dead and live and see?

Maid

It has felled her, and the life is breaking from her now.

Chorus

Such a husband, to lose such a wife. I pity you.

Maid

The master does not see it and he will not see it
until it happens.

Chorus

There is no hope left she will live?

Maid

None. This is the day of destiny. It is too strong.

Chorus

Surely, he must be doing all he can for her.

Maid

All is prepared so he can bury her in style.

Chorus

Let her be sure, at least, that as she dies, there dies
the noblest woman underneath the sun, by far.

Maid

Noblest? Of course the noblest, who will argue that?
What shall the wife be who surpasses her? And how

could any woman show that she loves her husband more
than herself better than by consent to die for him?
But all the city knows that well. You shall be told
now how she acted in the house, and be amazed
to hear. For when she understood the fatal day
was come, she bathed her white body with water drawn
from running streams, then opened the cedar chest and took
her clothes out, and dressed in all her finery
and stood before the Spirit in the Hearth, and prayed:
"Mistress, since I am going down beneath the ground,
I kneel before you in this last of all my prayers.
Take care of my children for me. Give the little girl
a husband; give the little boy a generous wife;
and do not let my children die like me, who gave
them birth, untimely. Let them live a happy life
through to the end and prosper here in their own land."
Afterward she approached the altars, all that stand
in the house of Admetus, made her prayers, and decked them all
with fresh sprays torn from living myrtle. And she wept
not at all, made no outcry. The advancing doom
made no change in the color and beauty of her face.
But then, in their room, she threw herself upon the bed,
and there she did cry, there she spoke: "O marriage bed,
it was here that I undressed my maidenhood and gave
myself up to this husband for whose sake I die.
Goodbye. I hold no grudge. But you have been my death
and mine alone. I could not bear to play him false.
I die. Some other woman will possess you now.
She will not be better, but she might be happier."
She fell on the bed and kissed it. All the coverings
were drenched in the unchecked outpouring of her tears;
but after much crying, when all her tears were shed,
she rolled from the couch and walked away with eyes cast down,
began to leave the room, but turned and turned again
to fling herself once more upon the bed. Meanwhile
the children clung upon their mother's dress, and cried,

until she gathered them into her arms, and kissed
first one and then the other, as in death's farewell.
And all the servants in the house were crying now
in sorrow for their mistress. Then she gave her hand
to each, and each one took it, there was none so mean
in station that she did not stop and talk with him.
This is what Admetus and the house are losing. Had
he died, he would have lost her, but in this escape
he will keep the pain. It will not ever go away.

Chorus

Admetus surely must be grieving over this
when such a wife must be taken away from him.

Maid

Oh yes, he is crying. He holds his wife close in his arms,
imploring her not to forsake him. What he wants
is impossible. She is dying. The sickness fades her now.
She has gone slack, just an inert weight on the arm.
Still, though so little breath of life is left in her,
she wants to look once more upon the light of the sun,
since this will be the last time of all, and never again.
She must see the sun's shining circle yet one more time.
Now I must go announce your presence. It is not
everyone who bears so much good will toward our kings
as to stand by ready to help in their distress.
But you have been my master's friends since long ago.

(*Exit.*)

Chorus

O Zeus, Zeus, what way out of this evil
is there, what escape from this
which is happening to our princes?
A way, any way? Must I cut short my hair
for grief, put upon me the black
costume that means mourning?
We must, friends, clearly we must; yet still

let us pray to the gods. The gods
have power beyond all power elsewhere.

Paean, my lord,
Apollo, make some way of escape for Admetus.
Grant it, oh grant it. Once you found
rescue in him. Be now
in turn his redeemer from death.
Oppose bloodthirsty Hades.

Admetus,
O son of Pheres, what a loss
to suffer, when such a wife goes.
A man could cut his throat for this, for this
and less he could bind the noose upon his neck
and hang himself. For this is
not only dear, but dearest of all,
this wife you will see dead
on this day before you.

(Alcestis is carried from the house on a litter, supported by Admetus and followed by her children and servants of the household.)

But see, see,
she is coming out of the house and her husband is with her.
Cry out aloud, mourn, you land
of Pherae for the bravest
of wives fading in sickness and doomed
to the Death God of the world below.

I will never again say that marriage brings
more pleasure than pain. I judge by what
I have known in the past, and by seeing now
what happens to our king, who is losing a wife
brave beyond all others, and must live a life
that will be no life for the rest of time.

Alcestis

Sun, and light of the day,
O turning wheel of the sky, clouds that fly.

Admetus

The sun sees you and me, two people suffering,
who never hurt the gods so they should make you die.

Alcestis

My land, and palace arching my land,
and marriage chambers of Iolcus, my own country.

Admetus

Raise yourself, my Alcestis, do not leave me now.
I implore the gods to pity you. They have the power.

Alcestis

I see him there at the oars of his little boat in the lake,
the ferryman of the dead,
Charon, with his hand upon the oar,
and he calls me now: "What keeps you?
Hurry, you hold us back." He is urging me on
in angry impatience.

Admetus

The crossing you speak of is a bitter one for me;
ill starred; it is unfair we should be treated so.

Alcestis

Somebody has me, somebody takes me away, do you see,
don't you see, to the courts
of dead men. He frowns from under dark
brows. He has wings. It is Death.
Let me go, what are you doing, let go.
Such is the road
most wretched I have to walk.

Admetus

Sorrow for all who love you, most of all for me
and for the children. All of us share in this grief.

Alcestis

Let me go now, let me down,
flat. I have no strength to stand.

Death is close to me.
The darkness creeps over my eyes. O children,
my children, you have no mother now,
not any longer. Daylight is yours,
my children. Look on it and be happy.

Admetus

Ah, a bitter word for me to hear,
heavier than any death of my own.
Before the gods, do not be so harsh
as to leave me, leave your children forlorn.
No, up, and fight it.
There would be nothing left of me if you died.
All rests in you, our life, our not
having life. Your love is our worship.

Alcestis

Admetus, you can see how it is with me. Therefore,
I wish to have some words with you before I die.
I put you first, and at the price of my own life
made certain you would live and see the daylight. So
I die, who did not have to die, because of you.
I could have taken any man in Thessaly
I wished and lived in queenly state here in this house.
But since I did not wish to live bereft of you
and with our children fatherless, I did not spare
my youth, although I had so much to live for. Yet
your father, and the mother who bore you, gave you up,
though they had reached an age when it was good to die
and good to save their son and end it honorably.
You were their only one, and they had no more hope
of having other children if you died. That way
I would be living and you would live the rest of our time,
and you would not be alone and mourning for your wife
and tending motherless children. No, but it must be
that some god has so wrought that things shall be this way.
So be it. But swear now to do, in recompense,

what I shall ask you—not enough, oh, never enough,
since nothing is enough to make up for a life,
but fair, and you yourself will say so, since you love
these children as much as I do; or at least you should.
Keep them as masters in my house, and do not marry
again and give our children to a stepmother
who will not be so kind as I, who will be jealous
and raise her hand to your children and mine. Oh no,
do not do that, do not. That is my charge to you.
For the new-come stepmother hates the children born
to a first wife, no viper could be deadlier.
The little boy has his father for a tower of strength.
[He can talk with him and be spoken to in turn.]
But you, my darling, what will your girlhood be like,
how will your father's new wife like you? She must not
make shameful stories up about you, and contrive
to spoil your chance of marriage in the blush of youth,
because your mother will not be there to help you
when you are married, not be there to give you strength
when your babies are born, when only a mother's help will do.
For I must die. It will not be tomorrow, not
the next day, or this month, the horrible thing will come,
but now, at once, I shall be counted among the dead.
Goodbye, be happy, both of you. And you, my husband,
can boast the bride you took made you the bravest wife,
and you, children, can say, too, that your mother was brave.

Chorus

Fear nothing; for I dare to speak for him. He will
do all you ask. If he does not, the fault is his.

Admetus

It shall be so, it shall be, do not fear, since you
were mine in life, you still shall be my bride in death
and you alone, no other girl in Thessaly
shall ever be called wife of Admetus in your place.
There is none such, none so marked out in pride of birth

nor beauty's brilliance, nor in anything else. I have
these children, they are enough; I only pray the gods
grant me the bliss to keep them as we could not keep you.
I shall go into mourning for you, not for just
a year, but all my life while it still lasts, my dear,
and hate the woman who gave me birth always, detest
my father. These were called my own people. They were not.
You gave what was your own and dear to buy my life
and saved me. Am I not to lead a mourning life
when I have lost a wife like you? I shall make an end
of revelry and entertainment in my house,
the flowers and the music that were found here once.
No, I shall never touch the lutestrings ever again
nor have the heart to play music upon the flute
of Libya, for you took my joy in life with you.
I shall have the skilled hand of an artificer
make me an image of you to set in my room,
pay my devotions to it, hold it in my arms
and speak your name, and clasp it close against my heart,
and think I hold my wife again, though I do not,
cold consolation, I know it, and yet even so
I might drain the weight of sorrow. You could come
to see me in my dreams and comfort me. For they
who love find a time's sweetness in the visions of night.
Had I the lips of Orpheus and his melody
to charm the maiden daughter of Demeter and
her lord, and by my singing win you back from death,
I would have gone beneath the earth, and not the hound
of Pluto could have stayed me, not the ferryman
of ghosts, Charon at his oar. I would have brought you back
to life. Wait for me, then, in that place, till I die,
and make ready the room where you will live with me,
for I shall have them bury me in the same chest
as you, and lay me at your side, so that my heart
shall be against your heart, and never, even in death
shall I go from you. You alone were true to me.

Chorus

And I, because I am your friend and you
are mine, shall help you bear this sorrow, as I should.

Alcestis

Children, you now have heard your father promise me
that he will never marry again and not inflict
a new wife on you, but will keep my memory.

Admetus

I promise. I will keep my promise to the end.

Alcestis

On this condition, take the children. They are yours.

Admetus

I take them, a dear gift from a dear hand.

Alcestis

And now
you must be our children's mother, too, instead of me.

Admetus

I must be such, since they will no longer have you.

Alcestis

O children, this was my time to live, and I must go.

Admetus

Ah me, what shall I do without you all alone.

Alcestis

Time will soften it. The dead count for nothing at all.

Admetus

Oh, take me with you, for God's love, take me there too.

Alcestis

No, I am dying in your place. That is enough.

Admetus

O God, what a wife you are taking away from me.

Alcestis

It is true. My eyes darken and the heaviness comes.

Admetus

But I am lost, dear, if you leave me.

Alcestis

There is no use
in talking to me any more. I am not there.

Admetus

No, lift your head up, do not leave your children thus.

Alcestis

I do not want to, but it is goodbye, children.

Admetus

Look at them, oh look at them.

Alcestis

No. There is nothing more.

Admetus

Are you really leaving us?

Alcestis

Goodbye.

Admetus

Oh, I am lost.

Chorus

It is over now. Admetus' wife is gone from us.

Boy

O wicked fortune. Mother has gone down there,
father, she is not here with us
in the sunshine any more.
She was cruel and went away
and left me to live all alone.
Look at her eyes, look at her hands, so still.
Hear me, mother, listen to me, oh please,
listen, it is I, mother,
I your little one lean and kiss
your lips, and cry out to you.

Admetus

She does not see, she does not hear you. You and I
both have a hard and heavy load to carry now.

Boy

Father, I am too small to be left alone
by the mother I loved so much. Oh,
it is hard for me to bear
all this that is happening,
and you, little sister, suffer
with me too. Oh, father,
your marriage was empty, empty, she did not live
to grow old with you.
She died too soon. Mother, with you gone away,
the whole house is ruined.

(*Alcestis is carried into the house, followed by children and servants.*)

Chorus

Admetus, you must stand up to misfortune now.
You are not the first, and not the last of humankind
to lose a good wife. Therefore, you must understand
death is an obligation claimed from all of us.

Admetus

I understand it. And this evil which has struck
was no surprise. I knew about it long ago,
and knowledge was hard. But now, since we must bury our dead,
stay with me and stand by me, chant responsively
the hymn of the unsacrificed-to god below.
To all Thessalians over whom my rule extends
I ordain a public mourning for my wife, to be
observed with shaving of the head and with black robes.
The horses that you drive in chariots and those
you ride single shall have their manes cut short with steel,
and there shall be no sound of flutes within the city,
no sound of lyres, until twelve moons have filled and gone;
for I shall never bury any dearer dead

than she, nor any who loved me better. She deserves
my thanks. She died for me, which no one else would do.

(*Exit into the house.*)

Chorus

O daughter of Pelias
my wish for you is a happy life
in the sunless chambers of Hades.
Now let the dark-haired lord of Death himself, and the old man,
who sits at the steering oar
and ferries the corpses,
know that you are the bravest of wives, by far,
ever conveyed across the tarn
of Acheron in the rowboat.

Much shall be sung of you
by the men of music to the seven-strung mountain
lyre-shell, and in poems that have no music,
in Sparta when the season turns and the month Carneian
comes back, and the moon
rides all the night;
in Athens also, the shining and rich.
Such is the theme of song you left
in death, for the poets.

Oh that it were in my power
and that I had strength to bring you
back to light from the dark of death
with oars on the sunken river.
For you, O dearest among women, you only
had the hard courage
to give your life for your husband's and save
him from death. May the dust lie light
upon you, my lady. And should he now take
a new wife to his bed, he will win my horror and hatred,
mine, and your children's hatred too.

His mother would not endure
to have her body hidden in the ground

for him, nor the aged father.
He was theirs, but they had not courage to save him.
Oh shame, for the gray was upon them.
But you, in the pride
of youth, died for him and left the daylight.
May it only be mine to win
such wedded love as hers from a wife; for this
is given seldom to mortals; but were my wife such, I would have her
with me unhurt through her lifetime.

(*Enter Heracles from the road, travel-stained.*)

Heracles

My friends, people of Pherae and the villages
hereby, tell me, shall I find Admetus at home?

Chorus

Yes, Heracles, the son of Pheres is in the house.
But tell us, what is the errand that brings you here
to Thessaly and the city of Pherae once again?

Heracles

I have a piece of work to do for Eurystheus
of Tiryns.

Chorus

Where does it take you? On what far journey?

Heracles

To Thrace, to take home Diomedes' chariot.

Chorus

How can you? Do you know the man you are to meet?

Heracles

No. I have never been where the Bistones live.

Chorus

You cannot master his horses. Not without a fight.

Heracles

It is my work, and I cannot refuse.

Chorus

You must
kill him before you come back; or be killed and stay.

Heracles

If I must fight, it will not be for the first time.

Chorus

What good will it do you if you overpower their master?

Heracles

I will take the horses home to Tiryns and its king.

Chorus

It is not easy to put a bridle on their jaws.

Heracles

Easy enough, unless their nostrils are snorting fire.

Chorus

Not that, but they have teeth that tear a man apart.

Heracles

Oh no! Mountain beasts, not horses, feed like that.

Chorus

But you can see their mangers. They are caked with blood.

Heracles

And the man who raises them? Whose son does he claim he is?

Chorus

Ares'. And he is lord of the golden shield of Thrace.

Heracles

It sounds like my life and the kind of work I do.
It is a hard and steep way always that I go,
having to fight one after another all the sons
the war god ever got him, with Lycaon first,
again with Cycnus, and now here is a third fight
that I must have with the master of these horses. So—

I am Alcmene's son, and the man does not live
who will see me break before my enemy's attack.

Chorus

Here is the monarch of our country coming
from the house himself, Admetus.

(*Enter Admetus.*)

Admetus

Welcome and happiness
to you, O scion of Perseus' blood and child of Zeus.

Heracles

Happiness to you likewise, lord of Thessaly,
Admetus.

Admetus

I could wish it I know you mean well.

Heracles

What is the matter? Why is there mourning and cut hair?

Admetus

There is one dead here whom I must bury today.

Heracles

Not one of your children! I pray God shield them from that.

Admetus

Not they. My children are well and living in their house.

Heracles

If it is your father who is gone, his time was ripe.

Admetus

No, he is still there, Heracles. My mother, too.

Heracles

Surely you have not lost your wife, Alcestis.

Admetus

Yes
and no. There are two ways that I could answer that.

Heracles

Did you say that she is dead or that she is still alive?

Admetus

She is, but she is gone away. It troubles me.

Heracles

I still do not know what you mean. You are being obscure.

Admetus

You know about her and what must happen, do you not?

Heracles

I know that she has undertaken to die for you.

Admetus

How can she really live, then, when she has promised that?

Heracles

Ah, do not mourn her before she dies. Wait for the time.

Admetus

The point of death is death, and the dead are lost and gone.

Heracles

Being and nonbeing are considered different things.

Admetus

That is your opinion, Heracles. It is not mine.

Heracles

Well, but whose is the mourning now? Is it in the family?

Admetus

A woman. We were speaking of a woman, were we not?

Heracles

Was she a blood relative or someone from outside?

Admetus

No relation by blood, but she meant much to us.

Heracles

How does it happen that she died here in your house?

Admetus

She lost her father and came here to live with us.

Heracles

I am sorry,
Admetus. I wish I had found you in a happier state.

Admetus

Why do you say that? What do you mean to do?

Heracles

I mean
to go on, and stay with another of my friends.

Admetus

No, my lord, no. The evil must not come to that.

Heracles

The friend who stays with friends in mourning is in the way.

Admetus

The dead are dead. Go on in.

Heracles

No. It is always wrong
for guests to revel in a house where others mourn.

Admetus

There are separate guest chambers. We can take you there.

Heracles

Let me go, and I will thank you a thousand times.

Admetus

You shall not go to stay with any other man.
You there: open the guest rooms which are across the court
from the house, and tell the people who are there to provide
plenty to eat, and make sure that you close the doors

facing the inside court. It is not right for guests
to have their pleasures interrupted by sounds of grief.

(Heracles is ushered inside.)

Chorus

Admetus, are you crazy? What are you thinking of
to entertain guests in a situation like this?

Admetus

And if I had driven from my city and my house
the guest and friend who came to me, would you have approved
of me more? Wrong. My misery would still have been
as great, and I should be inhospitable too,
and there would be one more misfortune added to those
I have, if my house is called unfriendly to its friends.
For this man is my best friend, and he is my host
whenever I go to Argos, which is a thirsty place.

Chorus

Yes, but then why did you hide what is happening here
if this visitor is, as you say, your best friend?

Admetus

He would not have been willing to come inside my house
if he had known what trouble I was in. I know.
There are some will think I show no sense in doing this.
They will not like it. But my house does not know how
to push its friends away and not treat them as it should.

(He goes inside.)

Chorus

O liberal and forever free-handed house of this man,
the Pythian himself, lyric Apollo,
was pleased to live with you
and had patience upon your lands
to work as a shepherd,
and on the hill-folds and the slopes
piped to the pasturing of your flocks
in their season of mating.

And even dappled lynxes for delight in his melody
joined him as shepherds. From the cleft of Othrys descended
a red troop of lions,
and there, Phoebus, to your lyre's strain
there danced the bright-coated
fawn, adventuring from the deep
bearded pines, lightfooted for joy
in your song, in its kindness.

Therefore, your house is beyond
all others for wealth of flocks by the sweet waters
of Lake Boebias. For spread of cornland
and pasturing range its boundary stands
only there where the sun
stalls his horses in dark air by the Molossians.
Eastward he sways all to the harborless
Pelian coast on the Aegaean main.

Now he has spread wide his doors
and taken the guest in, when his eyes were wet
and he wept still for a beloved wife who died
in the house so lately. The noble strain
comes out, in respect for others.
All that wisdom means is there in the noble. I stand
in awe, and good hope has come again to my heart
that for this godly man the end will be good.

(Enter Admetus from the house, followed by servants with a covered litter.)

Admetus

Gentlemen of Pherae, I am grateful for your company.
My men are bearing to the burning place and grave
our dead, who now has all the state which is her due.
Will you then, as the custom is among us, say
farewell to the dead as she goes forth for the last time?

Chorus

Yes, but I see your father coming now. He walks

as old men do, and followers carry in their hands
gifts for your wife, to adorn her in the underworld.

(*Enter Pheres, attended, from outside.*)

Pheres

I have come to bear your sorrows with you, son. I know,
nobody will dispute it, you have lost a wife
both good and modest in her ways. Nevertheless,
you have to bear it, even though it is hard to bear.
Accept these gifts to deck her body, bury them
with her. Oh yes, she well deserves honor in death.
She died to save your life, my son. She would not let
me be a childless old man, would not let me waste
away in sorrowful age deprived of you. Thereby,
daring this generous action, she has made the life
of all women become a thing of better repute
than it was.
O you who saved him, you who raised us up
when we were fallen, farewell, even in Hades' house
may good befall you.
I say people ought to marry women
like this. Otherwise, better not to marry at all.

Admetus

I never invited you to come and see her buried,
nor do I count your company as that of a friend.
She shall not wear anything that you bring her.
She needs nothing from you to be buried in. Your time
to share my sorrow was when I was about to die.
But you stood out of the way and let youth take my place
in death, though you were old. Will you cry for her now?
It cannot be that my body ever came from you,
nor did the woman who claims she bore me and is called
my mother give me birth. I was got from some slave
and surreptitiously put to your wife to nurse.
You show it. Your nature in the crisis has come out.
I do not count myself as any child of yours.

Oh, you outpass the cowardice of all the world,
you at your age, come to the very last step of life
and would not, dared not, die for your own child. Oh, no,
you let this woman, married into our family,
do it instead, and therefore it is right for me
to call her all the father and mother that I have.
And yet you two should honorably have striven for
the right of dying for your child. The time of life
you had left for your living was short, in any case,
and she and I would still be living out our time
and I should not be hurt and grieving over her.
And yet, all that a man could have to bless his life
you have had. You had your youth in kingship. There was I
your son, ready to take it over, keep your house
in order, so you had no childless death to fear,
with the house left to be torn apart by other claims.
You cannot justify your leaving me to death
on grounds that I disrespected your old age. Always I
showed all consideration. See what thanks I get
from you and from the woman who gave me birth. Go on,
get you other children, you cannot do it too soon,
who will look after your old age, and lay you out
when you are dead, and see you buried properly.
I will not do it. This hand will never bury you.
I am dead as far as you are concerned, and if, because
I found another savior, I still look on the sun,
I count myself that person's child and fond support.
It is meaningless, the way the old men pray for death
and complain of age and the long time they have to live.
Let death only come close, not one of them still wants
to die. Their age is not a burden any more.

Chorus

Stop, stop. We have trouble enough already, child.
You will exasperate your father with this talk.

Pheres

Big words, son. Who do you think you are cursing out
like this? Some Lydian slave, some Phrygian that you bought?
I am a free Thessalian noble, nobly born
from a Thessalian. Are you forgetting that? You go
too far with your high-handedness. You volley brash
words at me, and fail to hit me, and then run away.
I gave you life, and made you master of my house,
and raised you. I am not obliged to die for you.
I do not acknowledge any tradition among us
that fathers should die for their sons. That is not Greek.
Your natural right is to find your own happiness
or unhappiness. All you deserve from me, you have.
You are lord of many. I have wide estates of land
to leave you, just as my father left them to me.
What harm have I done you then? What am I taking away
from you? Do not die for me, I will not die for you.
You like the sunlight. Don't you think your father does?
I count the time I have to spend down there as long,
and the time to live is little, but that little is sweet.
You fought shamelessly for a way to escape death,
and passed your proper moment, and are still alive
because you killed her. Then, you wretch, you dare to call
me coward, when you let your woman outdare you,
and die for her magnificent young man? I see.
You have found a clever scheme by which you *never* will die.
You will always persuade the wife you have at the time
to die for you instead. And you, so low, then dare
blame your own people for not wanting to do this.
Silence. I tell you, as you cherish your own life,
all other people cherish theirs. And if you call
us names, you will be called names, and the names are true.

Chorus

Too much evil has been said in this speech and in
that spoken before. Old sir, stop cursing your own son.

Admetus

No, speak, and I will speak too. If it hurts to hear
the truth, you should not have made a mistake with me.

Pheres

I should have made a mistake if I had died for you.

Admetus

Is it the same thing to die old and to die young?

Pheres

Yes. We have only one life and not two to live.

Admetus

I think you would like to live a longer time than Zeus.

Pheres

Cursing your parents, when they have done nothing to you?

Admetus

Yes, for I found you much in love with a long life.

Pheres

Who is it you are burying? Did not someone die?

Admetus

And that she died, you foul wretch, proves your cowardice.

Pheres

You cannot say that we were involved in her death.

Admetus

Ah.
I hope that some day you will stand in need of me.

Pheres

Go on, and court more women, so they all can die.

Admetus

Your fault. You were not willing to.

Pheres

No, I was not.
It is a sweet thing, this God's sunshine, sweet to see.

Admetus

That is an abject spirit, not a man's.

Pheres

You shall
not mock an old man while you carry out your dead.

Admetus

You will die in evil memory, when you do die.

Pheres

I do not care what they say of me when I am dead.

Admetus

How old age loses all the sense of shame.

Pheres

She was
not shameless, you found; she was only innocent.

Admetus

Get out of here now and let me bury my dead.

Pheres

I'll go. You murdered her, and you can bury her.
But you will have her brothers still to face. You'll pay,
for Acastus is no longer counted as a man
unless he sees you punished for his sister's blood.

Admetus

Go and be damned, you and that woman who lives with you.
Grow old as you deserve, childless, although your son
still lives. You shall not come again under the same roof
with me. And if I had to proclaim by heralds that I
disowned my father's house, I should have so proclaimed.

(*Pheres goes off.*)

Now we, for we must bear the sorrow that is ours,
shall go, and lay her body on the burning place.

Chorus

Ah, cruel the price of your daring,

O generous one, O noble and brave,
farewell. May Hermes of the world below
and Hades welcome you. And if, even there,
the good fare best, may you have high honor
and sit by the bride of Hades.

(*The body is borne off, followed by Admetus, servants, and Chorus. Thus the stage is empty. Then enter, from the house, the servant who was put in charge of Heracles.*)

Servant

I have known all sorts of foreigners who have come in
from all over the world here to Admetus' house,
and I have served them dinner, but I never yet
have had a guest as bad as this to entertain.
In the first place, he could see the master was in mourning,
but inconsiderately came in anyway.
Then, he refused to understand the situation
and be content with anything we could provide,
but when we failed to bring him something, demanded it,
and took a cup with ivy on it in both hands
and drank the wine of our dark mother, straight, until
the flame of the wine went all through him, and heated him,
and then he wreathed branches of myrtle on his head
and howled, off key. There were two kinds of music now-
to hear, for while he sang and never gave a thought
to the sorrows of Admetus, we servants were mourning
our mistress; but we could not show before our guest
with our eyes wet. Admetus had forbidden that.
So now I have to entertain this guest inside,
this ruffian thief, this highwayman, whatever he is,
while she is gone away from the house, and I could not
say goodbye, stretch my hand out to her in my grief
for a mistress who was like a mother to all the house
and me. She gentled her husband's rages, saved us all
from trouble after trouble. Am I not then right
to hate this guest who has come here in our miseries?

(*Enter Heracles from the house, drunk, but not hopelessly so.*)

Heracles

You there, with the sad and melancholy face, what is
the matter with you? The servant who looks after guests
should be polite and cheerful and not scowl at them.
But look at you. Here comes your master's dearest friend
to visit you, and you receive him with black looks
and frowns, all because of some trouble somewhere else.
Come here, I'll tell you something that will make you wise.
Do you really know what things are like, the way they are?
I don't think so. How could you? Well then, listen to me.
Death is an obligation which we all must pay.
There is not one man living who can truly say
if he will be alive or dead on the next day.
Fortune is dark; she moves, but we cannot see the way
nor can we pin her down by science and study her.
There, I have told you. Now you can understand. Go on,
enjoy yourself, drink, call the life you live today
your own, but only that, the rest belongs to chance.
Then, beyond all gods, pay your best attentions to
the Cyprian, man's sweetest. There's a god who's kind.
Let all this business go and do as I prescribe
for you, that is, if I seem to talk sense. Do I?
I think so. Well, then, get rid of this too-much grief,
put flowers on your head and drink with us, fight down
these present troubles; later, I know very well
that the wine splashing in the bowl will shake you loose
from these scowl-faced looks and the tension in your mind.
We are only human. Our thoughts should be human too,
since, for these solemn people and these people who scowl,
the whole parcel of them, if I am any judge,
life is not really life but a catastrophe.

Servant

I know all that. But we have troubles on our hands
now, that make revelry and laughter out of place.

Heracles

The dead woman is out of the family. Do not mourn
too hard. The master and the mistress are still alive.

Servant

What do you mean, alive? Do you not know what happened?

Heracles

Certainly, unless your master has lied to me.

Servant

He is too hospitable, too much.

Heracles

Should I not then
have enjoyed myself, because some outside woman was dead?

Servant

She was an outsider indeed. That is too true.

Heracles

Has something happened that he did not tell me about?

Servant

Never mind. Go. Our masters' sorrows are our own.

Heracles

These can be no outsiders' troubles.

Servant

If they were,
I should not have minded seeing you enjoy yourself.

Heracles

Have I been scandalously misled by my own friends?

Servant

You came here when we were not prepared to take in guests.
You see, we are in mourning. You can see our robes
of black, and how our hair is cut short.

Heracles

Who is dead?
The aged father? One of the children who is gone?

Servant

My lord, Admetus' wife is dead.

Heracles

What are you saying?
And all this time you were making me comfortable?

Servant

He could not bear to turn you from this house of his.

Heracles

My poor Admetus, what a helpmeet you have lost!

Servant

We are all dead and done for now, not only she.

Heracles

I really knew it when I saw the tears in his eyes,
his shorn hair and his face; but he persuaded me
with talk of burying someone who was not by blood
related. So, unwillingly, I came inside
and drank here in the house of this hospitable man
when he was in this trouble! Worse, I wreathed my head
with garlands, and drank freely. But you might have said
something about this great disaster in the house.
Now, where shall I find her? Where is the funeral being held?

Servant

Go straight along the Larisa road, and when you clear
the city you will see the monument and the mound.

(*He goes into the house, leaving Heracles alone on the stage.*)

Heracles

O heart of mine and hand of mine, who have endured
so much already, prove what kind of son it was
Alcmene, daughter of Electryon, bore to Zeus
in Tiryns. I must save this woman who has died
so lately, bring Alcestis back to live in this house,
and pay Admetus all the kindness that I owe.
I must go there and watch for Death of the black robes,
master of dead men, and I think I shall find him

drinking the blood of slaughtered beasts beside the grave.
Then, if I can break suddenly from my hiding place,
catch him, and hold him in the circle of these arms,
there is no way he will be able to break my hold
on his bruised ribs, until he gives the woman up
to me. But if I miss my quarry, if he does not come
to the clotted offering, I must go down, I must ask
the Maiden and the Master in the sunless homes
of those below; and I have confidence I shall bring
Alcestis back, and give her to the arms of my friend
who did not drive me off but took me into his house
and, though he staggered under the stroke of circumstance,
hid it, for he was noble and respected me.
Who in all Thessaly is a truer friend than this?
Who in all Greece? Therefore, he must not ever say
that, being noble, he befriended a worthless man.

(*He goes out. Presently Admetus comes on, followed by the Chorus.*)

Admetus

Hateful is this
return, hateful the sight of this house
widowed, empty. Where shall I go?
Where shall I stay? What shall I say?
How can I die?
My mother bore me to a heavy fate.
I envy the dead. I long for those
who are gone, to live in their houses, with them.
There is no pleasure in the sunshine
nor the feel of the hard earth under my feet.
Such was the hostage Death has taken
from me, and given to Hades.

(*As they chant this, Admetus moans inarticulately.*)

Chorus

Go on, go on. Plunge in the deep of the house.
What you have suffered is enough for tears.
You have gone through pain, I know,

but you do no good to the woman who lies
below. Never again to look on the face
of the wife you loved hurts you.

Admetus

You have opened the wound torn in my heart.
What can be worse for a man than to lose
a faithful wife. I envy those
without wives, without children. I wish I had not
ever married her, lived with her in this house.
We have each one life. To grieve for this
is burden enough.
When we could live single all our days
without children, it is not to be endured
to see children sicken or married love
despoiled by death.

(*As before.*)

Chorus

Chance comes. It is hard to wrestle against it.
There is no limit to set on your pain.
The weight is heavy. Yet still
bear up. You are not the first man to lose
his wife. Disaster appears, to crush
one man now, but afterward another.

Admetus

How long my sorrows, the pain for my loves
down under the earth.
Why did you stop me from throwing myself
in the hollow cut of the grave, there to lie
dead beside her, who was best on earth?
Then Hades would have held fast two lives,
not one, and the truest of all, who crossed
the lake of the dead together.

Chorus

There was a man
of my people, who lost a boy

any house would mourn for,
the only child. But still
he carried it well enough, though childless,
and he stricken with age
and the hair gray on him,
well on through his lifetime.

Admetus

O builded house, how shall I enter you?
How live, with this turn
of my fortune? How different now and then.
Then it was with Pelian pine torches,
with marriage songs, that I entered my house,
with the hand of a sweet bride on my arm,
with loud rout of revelers following
to bless her who now is dead, and me,
for our high birth, for nobilities
from either side which were joined in us.
Now the bridal chorus has changed for a dirge,
and for white robes the costumed black
goes with me inside
to where her room stands deserted.

Chorus

Your luck had been
good, so you were inexperienced when
grief came. Still you saved
your own life and substance.
Your wife is dead, your love forsaken.
What is new in this? Before
now death has parted
many from their wives.

Admetus

Friends, I believe my wife is happier than I
although I know she does not seem to be. For her,
there will be no more pain to touch her ever again.

She has her glory and is free from much distress.
But I, who should not be alive, who have passed by
my moment, shall lead a sorry life. I see it now.
How can I bear to go inside this house again?
Whom shall I speak to, who will speak to me, to give
me any pleasure in coming home? Where shall I turn?
The desolation in my house will drive me out
when I see my wife's bed empty, when I see the chairs
she used to sit in, and all about the house the floor
unwashed and dirty, while the children at my knees
huddle and cry for their mother and the servants mourn
their mistress and remember what the house has lost.
So it will be at home, but if I go outside
meeting my married friends in Thessaly, the sight
of their wives will drive me back, for I cannot endure
to look at my wife's agemates and the friends of her youth.
And anyone who hates me will say this of me:
"Look at the man, disgracefully alive, who dared
not die, but like a coward gave his wife instead
and so escaped death. Do you call him a man at all?
He turns on his own parents, but he would not die
himself." Besides my other troubles, they will speak
about me thus. What have I gained by living, friends,
when reputation, life, and action all are bad?

Chorus

I myself, in the transports
of mystic verses, as in study
of history and science, have found
nothing so strong as Compulsion,
nor any means to combat her,
not in the Thracian books set down
in verse by the school of Orpheus,
not in all the remedies Phoebus has given the heirs
of Asclepius to fight the many afflictions of man.

She alone is a goddess
without altar or image to pray

before. She heeds no sacrifice.
Majesty, bear no harder
on me than you have in my life before!
All Zeus even ordains
only with you is accomplished.
By strength you fold and crumple the steel of the Chalybes.
There is no pity in the sheer barrier of your will.

(*They turn and speak directly to Admetus, who remains in the background.*)

Now she has caught your wife in the breakless grip of her hands.
Take it. You will never bring back, by crying,
the dead into the light again.
Even the sons of the gods fade
and go in death's shadow.
She was loved when she was with us.
She shall be loved still, now she is dead.
It was the best of all women to whom you were joined in marriage.

The monument of your wife must not be counted among the graves
of the dead, but it must be given its honors
as gods are, worship of wayfarers.
And as they turn the bend of the road
and see it, men shall say:
"She died for the sake of her husband.
Now she is a blessed spirit.
Hail, majesty, be gracious to us." Thus will men speak in her presence.

But here is someone who looks like Alcmene's son,
Admetus. He seems on his way to visit you.

(*Heracles enters, leading a veiled woman by the hand.*)

Heracles

A man, Admetus, should be allowed to speak his mind
to a friend, instead of keeping his complaints suppressed
inside him. Now, I thought I had the right to stand

beside you and endure what you endured, so prove
my friendship. But you never told me that she, who lay
dead, was your wife, but entertained me in your house
as if your mourning were for some outsider's death.
And so I wreathed my head and poured libations out
to the gods, in your house, though your house had suffered so.
This was wrong, wrong I tell you, to have treated me
thus, though I have no wish to hurt you in your grief.
Now, as for the matter of why I have come back again,
I will tell you. Take this woman, keep her safe for me,
until I have killed the master of the Bistones
and come back, bringing with me the horses of Thrace.
If I have bad luck—I hope not, I hope to come
back home—I give her to the service of your house.
It cost a struggle for her to come into my hands.
You see, I came on people who were holding games
for all comers, with prizes which an athlete might
well spend an effort winning.

(Points to the woman.)

Here is the prize I won
and bring you. For the winners in the minor events
were given horses to take away, while those who won
the heavier stuff, boxing and wrestling, got oxen,
and a woman was thrown in with them. Since I happened
to be there, it seemed wrong to let this splendid prize
go by. As I said, the woman is for you to keep.
She is not stolen. It cost me hard work to bring
her here. Some day, perhaps, you will say I have done well.

Admetus

I did not mean to dishonor nor belittle you
when I concealed the fate of my unhappy wife,
but it would have added pain to pain already there
if you had been driven to shelter with some other host.
This sorrow is mine. It is enough for me to weep.
As for the woman, if it can be done, my lord,

I beg you, have some other Thessalian, who has not
suffered as I have, keep her. You have many friends
in Pherae. Do not bring my sorrows back to me.
I would not have strength to see her in my house and keep
my eyes dry. I am weak now. Do not add weakness
to my weakness. I have sorrow enough to weigh me down.
And where could a young woman live in this house? For
she is young, I can see it in her dress, her style.
Am I to put her in the same quarters with the men?
And how, circulating among young men, shall she be kept
from harm? Not easy, Heracles, to hold in check
a young strong man. I am thinking of your interests.
Or shall I put her in my lost wife's chamber, keep
her there? How can I take her to Alcestis' bed?
I fear blame from two quarters, from my countrymen
who might accuse me of betraying her who helped
me most, by running to the bed of another girl,
and from the dead herself. Her honor has its claim
on me. I must be very careful. You, lady,
whoever you are, I tell you that you have the form
of my Alcestis; all your body is like hers.
Too much. Oh, for God's pity, take this woman away
out of my sight. I am beaten already, do not beat
me again. For as I look on her, I think I see
my wife. It churns my heart to tumult, and the tears
break streaming from my eyes. How much must I endure
the bitter taste of sorrow which is still so fresh?

Chorus

I cannot put a good name to your fortune; yet
whoever you are, you must endure what the god gives.

Heracles

I only wish that my strength had been great enough
for me to bring your wife back from the chambered deep
into the light. I would have done that grace for you.

Admetus

I know you would have wanted to. Why speak of it?
There is no way for the dead to come back to the light.

Heracles

Then do not push your sorrow. Bear it as you must.

Admetus

Easier to comfort than to suffer and be strong.

Heracles

But if you wish to mourn for always, what will you gain?

Admetus

Nothing. I know it. But some impulse of my love
makes me.

Heracles

Why, surely. Love for the dead is cause for tears.

Admetus

Her death destroyed me, even more than I can say.

Heracles

You have lost a fine wife. Who will say you have not?

Admetus

So fine
that I, whom you see, never shall be happy again.

Heracles

Time will soften it. The evil still is young and strong.

Admetus

You can say time will soften it, if time means death.

Heracles

A wife, love, your new marriage will put an end to this.

Admetus

Silence! I never thought you would say a thing like that.

Heracles

What? You will not remarry but keep an empty bed?

Admetus

No woman ever shall sleep in my arms again.

Heracles

Do you believe you help the dead by doing this?

Admetus

Wherever she may be, she deserves my honors still.

Heracles

Praiseworthy, yes, praiseworthy. And yet foolish, too.

Admetus

Call me so, then, but never call me a bridegroom.

Heracles

I admire you for your faith and love you bear your wife.

Admetus

Let me die if I betray her, though she is gone.

Heracles

Well then,
receive this woman into your most generous house.

Admetus

Please, in the name of Zeus your father, no!

Heracles

And yet
you will be making a mistake if you do not;

Admetus

and eaten at the heart with anguish if I do.

Heracles

Obey. The grace of this may come where you need grace.

Admetus

Ah.
I wish you had never won her in those games of yours.

Heracles

Where I am winner, you are winner along with me.

Admetus

Honorably said. But let the woman go away.

Heracles

She will go, if she should. First look. See if she should.

Admetus

She should, unless it means you will be angry with me.

Heracles

Something I know of makes me so insistent with you.

Admetus

So, have your way. But what you do does not please me.

Heracles

The time will come when you will thank me. Only obey.

Admetus (to attendants)

Escort her in, if she must be taken into this house.

Heracles

I will not hand this lady over to attendants.

Admetus

You yourself lead her into the house then, if you wish.

Heracles

I will put her into your hands and into yours alone.

Admetus

I will not touch her. But she is free to come inside.

Heracles

No, I have faith in your right hand, and only yours.

Admetus

My lord, you are forcing me to act against my wish.

Heracles

Be brave. Reach out your hand and take the stranger's.

Admetus

So.

Here is my hand; I feel like Perseus killing the gorgon.

Heracles

You have her?

Admetus

Yes, I have her.

Heracles

Keep her, then. Some day
you will say the son of Zeus came as your generous guest.
But look at her. See if she does not seem most like
your wife. Your grief is over now. Your luck is back.

Admetus

Gods, what shall I think! Amazement beyond hope, as I
look on this woman, this wife. Is she really mine,
or some sweet mockery for God to stun me with?

Heracles

Not so. This is your own wife you see. She is here.

Admetus

Be careful she is not some phantom from the depths.

Heracles

The guest and friend you took was no necromancer.

Admetus

Do I see my wife, whom I was laying in the grave?

Heracles

Surely. But I do not wonder at your unbelief.

Admetus

May I touch her, and speak to her, as my living wife?

Heracles

Speak to her. All that you desired is yours.

Admetus

Oh, eyes
and body of my dearest wife, I have you now
beyond all hope. I never thought to see you again.

Heracles

You have her. May no god hate you for your happiness.

Admetus

O nobly sprung child of all-highest Zeus, may good
fortune go with you. May the father who gave you birth
keep you. You alone raised me up when I was down.
How did you bring her back from down there to the light?

Heracles

I fought a certain deity who had charge of her.

Admetus

Where do you say you fought this match with Death?

Heracles

Beside
the tomb itself. I sprang and caught him in my hands.

Admetus

But why is my wife standing here, and does not speak?

Heracles

You are not allowed to hear her speak to you until
her obligations to the gods who live below
are washed away. Until the third morning comes. So now
take her and lead her inside, and for the rest of time,
Admetus, be just. Treat your guests as they deserve.
and now goodbye. I have my work that I must do,
and go to face the lordly son of Sthenelus.

Admetus

No, stay with us and be the guest of our hearth.

Heracles

There still
will be a time for that, but I must press on now.

Admetus

Success go with you. May you find your way back here.

(*Heracles goes.*)

I proclaim to all the people of my tetrarchy
that, for these blessed happenings, they shall set up
dances, and the altars smoke with sacrifice offered.

For now we shall make our life again, and it will be
a better one.
I was lucky. That I cannot deny.

(He takes Alcestis by the hand and leads her inside the house.)

Chorus (going)

Many are the forms of what is unknown.
Much that the gods achieve is surprise.
What we look for does not come to pass;
God finds a way for what none foresaw.
Such was the end of this story.

THE COMPLETE GREEK TRAGEDIES

AESCHYLUS · I *ORESTEIA*

Translated and with an Introduction by Richmond Lattimore

Agamemnon
The Libation Bearers
The Eumenides

AESCHYLUS · II *FOUR TRAGEDIES*

The Suppliant Maidens. *S. G. Benardete*
The Persians. *S. G. Benardete*
Seven against Thebes. *David Grene*
Prometheus Bound. *David Grene*

SOPHOCLES · I *THREE TRAGEDIES*

Translated and with an Introduction by David Grene

Oedipus the King
Oedipus at Colonus
Antigone

SOPHOCLES · II *FOUR TRAGEDIES*

Ajax. *John Moore*
The Women of Trachis. *Michael Jameson*
Electra *and* Philoctetes. *David Grene*

EURIPIDES · I *FOUR TRAGEDIES*

With an Introduction by Richmond Lattimore

Alcestis. *Richmond Lattimore*
The Medea. *Rex Warner*
The Heracleidae. *Ralph Gladstone*
Hippolytus. *David Grene*

EURIPIDES · II *FOUR TRAGEDIES*

The Cyclops *and* Heracles. *William Arrowsmith*
Iphigenia in Tauris. *Witter Bynner. Introduction by Richmond Lattimore*
Helen. *Richmond Lattimore*

EURIPIDES · III *FOUR TRAGEDIES*

Hecuba. *William Arrowsmith*
Andromache. *John Frederick Nims*
The Trojan Women. *Richmond Lattimore*
Ion. *R. F. Willetts*

EURIPIDES · IV *FOUR TRAGEDIES*

Rhesus. *Richmond Lattimore*
The Suppliant Women. *Frank William Jones*
Orestes. *William Arrowsmith*
Iphigenia in Aulis. *Charles R. Walker*

EURIPIDES · V *THREE TRAGEDIES*

Electra. *Emily Townsend Vermeule*
The Phoenician Women. *Elizabeth Wyckoff*
The Bacchae. *William Arrowsmith*